THE STUFF OF MANHOOD

By ROBERT E. SPEER

The Stuff of Manhood   12mo, cloth, net $1.00

John's Gospel, The Greatest Book in the World
                                  12mo, cloth, net 60c.

Men Who Were Found Faithful   12mo, cloth, net $1.00

Some Great Leaders in the World Movement
     The Cole Lectures for 1911.   12mo, cloth, net $1.25

The Foreign Doctor: "The Hakim Sahib"
     A Biography of Joseph Plumb Cochran, M.D., of Persia.
                    Illustrated, 12mo, cloth, net $1.50

Christianity and the Nations
     The Duff Lectures for 1910.   8vo, cloth, net $2.00

Missionary Principles and Practice 8vo, cloth, net $1.50

A Memorial of Alice Jackson   12mo, cloth, net 75c.

A Memorial of Horace Tracy Pitkin
                                  12mo, cloth, net $1.00

A Memorial of a True Life
     A Biography of Hugh McAllister Beaver With Portrait
                                  12mo, cloth, $1.00

Young Men Who Overcame   12mo, cloth, net $1.00

Paul, the All-Round Man   16mo, cloth, net 50c.

The Master of the Heart   12mo, cloth, net $1.00

A Young Man's Questions   12mo, cloth, net $1.00

The Principles of Jesus In Some Applications to Present
     Life   16mo, net 60c.

Christ and Life The Practice of the Christian Life
                                  12mo, cloth, net $1.00

Studies of the Man Paul   16mo, cloth, 75c.

Studies of "The Man Christ Jesus"   16mo, cloth, 75c.

Remember Jesus Christ And Other Talks About Christ
     and the Christian Life   16mo, cloth, 75c.

The Deity of Christ   18mo, boards, net 25c.

The Merrick Lectures for 1916-17. Delivered at the Ohio Wesleyan University, Delaware, Ohio, April 1-5, 1917

The Stuff of Manhood

SOME NEEDED NOTES IN AMERICAN CHARACTER

By
ROBERT E. SPEER

NEW YORK   CHICAGO   TORONTO

Fleming H. Revell Company

LONDON   AND   EDINBURGH

New York: 158 Fifth Avenue
Chicago: 17 North Wabash Ave.
Toronto: 25 Richmond Street, W.
London: 21 Paternoster Square
Edinburgh: 100 Princes Street

The Merrick Lectures

B Y the gift of the late Rev. Frederick
Merrick, M. D., D. D., LL. D., for fifty-
one years a member of the Faculty, and
for thirteen of those years President of Ohio
Wesleyan University, a fund was established
providing an annual income for the purpose of
securing lectures within the general field of
Experimental and Practical Religion. The following courses have previously been given on
this foundation :

Daniel Curry, D. D.—" Christian Education."

President James McCosh, D. D., LL. D.—
" Tests of the Various Kinds of Truth."

Bishop Randolph S. Foster, D. D., LL. D.—
" The Philosophy of Christian Experience."

Professor James Stalker, D. D.—"The Preacher
and His Models."

John W. Butler, D. D.—" Mission Work in
Mexico."

Professor George Adam Smith, D. D., LL. D.
—" Christ in the Old Testament."

Bishop James W. Bashford, Ph. D., D. D.,
LL. D.—" The Science of Religion."

James M. Buckley, D. D., LL. D.—" The Natural and Spiritual Orders and Their Relations."

John R. Mott, M. A., F. R. G. S.—" The Pastor and Modern Missions."

Bishop Elijah E. Hoss, D. D., LL. D.; Professor Doremus A. Hayes, Ph. D., S. T. D., LL. D.; Charles E. Jefferson, D. D., LL. D.; Bishop William F. McDowell, D. D., LL. D.; President Edwin H. Hughes, D. D.—" The New Age and Its Creed."

Robert E. Speer, M. A.—" The Marks of a Man, or The Essentials of Christian Character."

Rev. Charles Stelzle, Miss Jane Addams, Commissioner of Labor Charles P. Neill, Ph. D., Professor Graham Taylor, and Rev. George P. Eckman, D. D.—" The Social Application of Religion."

Rev. George Jackson, M. A.—" Some Old Testament Problems."

Professor Walter Rauschenbusch, D. D.— " Christianizing the Social Order."

Professor G. A. Johnston Ross, M. A.—" One Avenue of Faith."

Introduction

THE moral elements of individual character are inevitably social. And the social obligation immensely strengthens the sanctions which enjoin them. When a man "has trained himself," to use the words of Lord Morley in dealing with Voltaire's religion, "to look upon every wrong in thought, every duty omitted from act, each infringement of the inner spiritual law which humanity is constantly perfecting for its own guidance and advantage . . . as an ungrateful infection, weakening and corrupting the future of his brothers," he views each struggle within his own soul against evil and each firm aspiration after purity not as a mere incident in his own spiritual biography but as a fight for social good and for the perfecting of the nation and of humanity. And the struggle for social good and the perfecting of human life is fundamentally a struggle for the triumph of ideals in personal wills. God can take hold of men only in man. He revealed Himself and wrought redemption less by a social process than by a personal incarnation. And the only way of which we know to uplift the life of the nation and to fit it for its mission and its ministry is to reform our own and other men's characters, and ourselves to be what manner of man among men we would have the nation be among nations. It is of some of the elements of character of which men stand specially in need to-day that we are to speak in these lectures. What is good in our lives as individuals and in our life as a nation is not in need of discussion here. And there is no nobility in analyzing and deriding our weaknesses. Our purpose is to urge our keeping if we have not lost them, and our regaining if we feel them slipping from us, some of the elemental moral qualities and spiritual resources which are vital to the capacity for duty and to the living of a full and efficient life.

It has seemed best, on the whole, to preserve in the printed volume the free colloquialism of the lectures as they were delivered.

R. E. S.

New York.

Contents

LECTURE I

DISCIPLINE AND AUSTERITY

WHETHER there should be compulsory military training in America is a question which some people will answer yes or no according to their general theories and others according to their observation of the actual effects of such training on moral character. But whatever our views may be on this familiar question, whether we regard military service as ethically helpful in its influence or as morally injurious, we cannot differ as to the need in our national character of those qualities of self-control, of quick and unquestioning obedience to duty, of joyful contempt of hardship, and of zest in difficult and arduous undertakings which, rightly or wrongly, we consider soldierly, which we attribute in such rich measure to our forefathers, and which the moral exigencies of our national task to-day as peremptorily demand. To put these primary and elemental needs as sharply as possible, let us call them discipline and austerity. Our American character needs more of both.

I do not know a better starting point than is found in one of those vivid modern touches upon which we constantly come in the Old Testament. This one is in the account of the closing year of King David's life. The story seems ancient and far away until we suddenly read : "His father had not displeased him at any time saying, Why hast thou done so ?" If we were to translate the words more directly into the language of our own day, we should say, "His father had always let him do exactly as he pleased." The reference is to David and his son Adonijah, and to the want of discipline by which the father had ruined his boy.

It is not hard to reconstruct the story. David was busy about his cares as king, and his heart was indulgent towards his children. Adonijah seems to have been his youngest son, and the father let him have his way, never reining him up or checking him by asking why he had done thus or so. David pursued, in other words, the modern theory of child training : that the one principle by which children should be educated is the principle of letting what is naturally in them come out ; that they must not be crossed or frustrated, or have any external discipline or control laid upon their lives. This is, of course, the extreme of it, but in some form we hear the theory and see it applied all about us every day.

And it is a modern theory of self-education, also. We are told that life should be left free to follow its native impulses ; that it should not be thwarted and intimidated by the conventions and prohibitions of society ; that men and women should consult their own hearts and then should move out quite freely in obedience to their promptings ; that their lives and the lives of their children should not be twisted or deflected by the imposition of any external authority or command.

Well, that was the way Adonijah was brought up. His father was rich. The boy had his own establishment, his own horses, his own retinue of attendants, and round about him, as about any oriental king's son, there would be the usual crowd of flatterers and sycophants. There was no will or desire that he had not the means to gratify, and his father let him have his way.

Further, he was the younger brother of Absalom, and the ancient record says that they were handsome and popular boys. They had a way that carried along those who came in touch with them, and as the king's sons, and the leading young men of the city, we have no difficulty in understanding the atmosphere in which they lived and the conditions within which they grew.

It must be confessed that this was the easy way of going about the matter. It is far easier to let a child have its own way than to endeavour by wisdom and patience and strength, to study and decide what is best for the child and without hurting the child's will, to guide it into the better way. It was far less care to David to let Absalom and Adonijah go than it would have been to take these high-strung sons of his in hand and endeavour to break them to discipline and truth, and to send them out into life real men of power. It was much easier never to call them and to say, " Boys, why did you do this ? " Much easier never to lay any authority or guidance upon them from without, much easier, especially for a man like David. He had grown up on a farm, with all the hardship and frugality of farm life, with no privileges as a lad, and now that he was the king of his nation, he was able to do anything whatever for his sons. It was difficult to refuse them the things he had never had. Easily and indulgently—for he was a man of kindly heart all his days—he found it simpler not to lay hard restraints upon his boys when he could give them their own way.

And, of course, this is the easier way of self-education too. For a man to love himself so much that he never thinks of his neighbours, to blind his eyes so completely to consequences that he can live for the passing moment,—this is a very easy philosophy, and the man or the woman who is able to practice it will seem, for a while, to live in the sunshine, a fine butterfly, smooth-going life. All this is easier than to say, not, What is my impulse? but, What ought I? not, What do I like? but, What is best for all the world? not, What is the easy way? but,

What is the hard way over which the feet go that carry the burdens of mankind, that bear the load of the world?

But, though it is the easy way for a while, there comes a time when it is no longer the easy way. When in his little room above the gate the old king bowed his gray head in his hands and with breaking heart sobbed out: " O my son Absalom! my son, my son Absalom! would God I had died for thee, O Absalom, my son, my son!"—it was no longer the easy way. When Adonijah rose up in insurrection against his old father as he lay on his dying bed, gathering his little company of sycophants around him and setting himself up in his father's place, then it was no longer the easy way that the old man had pursued.

And to-day still, fathers and mothers who for a little while thought the easy way was never to ask their children why they had done so, but to let them go their own way with no imposition of outward authority or control, find after a while that tne easy way has turned bitterly hard. I have a friend, a leading merchant in one of our large cities. Some time ago another friend was visiting him, and as they walked down the street together, suddenly a large car whizzed around the corner, full of young people, among them the merchant's son. This was the middle of the forenoon and the boy was supposed to be at work in his father's establishment.   The father turned to his friend and said: "I wish I knew how I could hold my boy in."   But my friend understood why he could not.   He knew that only two or three years before the son had been rewarded for passing examinations at college, examinations that it ought to have been taken for granted that he would pass.   But his father thought he should be rewarded for passing them, and he bought a car and sent it up to him at college.   Now he wonders why this son does not know how to bind himself to arduous duty.

And in our own lives the easy education does not go easily all the way.   There comes a time when, having always indulged ourselves, we can't break the habit; when, never having taken our lives in our hands and reined them to the great ministries of mankind, we discover that we cannot. We find that we obey our caprices; follow any impulse; cannot stick to any task; do not know a principle when we see it; have no iron or steel anywhere in our character; are the riffraff of the world that the worthy men and women have to bear along as they go.   In Mr. Kipling's inelegant lines:

" We was rotten 'fore we started—we was never
        disci*plined;*
    We made it out a favour if an order was obeyed;
    Yes, every little drummer 'ad 'is rights and wrongs
        to mind,
    So we had to pay for teachin'—an' we paid!"

Now I suggest that we put all this positively to ourselves, for every one of us knows that we are treading near some of the moral realities of weakness and need in our day and nation. Why should restraint, obedience, the authority of duty and God be let into our lives? In order that out of all these things self-control may come. And why should there be this submission and control of our lives by duty, and truth and God? Well, the reasons are obvious, the moment we begin to think about them.

There is the indisputable fact that the strongest and best men and women we know are men and women who were trained in this school, who some time during their life, and the earlier the better, passed under the discipline and influence of that chastening spoken about in the twelfth chapter of the Epistle to the Hebrews, without which we are not children of a clean God. All around us are these men and women, fathers and mothers, who indulge their sons and daughters, who never confront them with moral principle and obligation and duty, and then lament because their children do not seem to have the old iron grasp of duty, the old rigid love of truth and righteousness. Well, it is all very simple. It is because those fathers and mothers are denying to their children the very education that made themselves what they are. The men and women, who will not run away from any task, who stand steadfast in the truth, upon whose every word we can rest our whole soul, grew out of a certain discipline, a certain education, and it was the kind that Adonijah did not have. And all men and women who want to be masters of their lives and to have strength to lay beneath the work of the world must ask God that such discipline may be given to them.

Not alone is this the only kind of training that can produce this kind of character, but unless a man learns control from without, he will never learn self-control. Unless he passes under the discipline of a wiser and stronger hand at the beginning, he will never come to the time of deliberate and moral self-discipline, which alone is character. For this only is character,—the binding of life beneath the firm sovereignty of the principle that is the heart of God. If nations do not realize this they will pay heavily for their failure. "Make your educational laws strict," said Ruskin, "and your criminal laws may be gentle; but leave youth its liberty and you will have to dig dungeons for age."

And it is this that gives freedom. There is no freedom outside of character. Liberty, as Montesquieu says, is not freedom to do just as we please. Liberty is the ability to do as we ought. And the freedom that we need is not the freedom of caprice and whim and listening to our impulses. It is the freedom that enables our eyes clearly to see what right is, and then empowers us to do it.   Symonds put it in his verse:

> " Soul, rule thyself.   On passion, deed, desire,
>   Lay thou the law of thy deliberate will.
>   Stand at thy chosen post, faith's sentinel.
>   Learn to endure.   Thine the reward
>   Of those who make living light their Lord.
>   Clad with celestial steel these stand secure,
>   Masters, not slaves."

And if such self-control goes as far even as the self-extinction of that voluntarily accepted Cross, on the green hill outside Jerusalem, even so it will bring victory at the last, because it has brought one long succession of victories over self all the days.   I cut this fugitive bit of verse from a newspaper the other day:

> " Pausing a moment ere the day was done,
>   While yet the earth was scintillant with light,
>   I backward glanced.   From valley, plain and height,
>   At intervals, where my life path had run,
>   Rose cross on cross: and nailed upon each one
>   Was my dead self.   And yet that gruesome sight
>   Lent sudden splendour to the falling night.
>   Showing the conquests that my soul had won.
>
> " Up to the rising stars I looked and cried,
>   There is no death !   For year on year reborn,
>   I wake to larger life, to joy more great.
>   So many times have I been crucified,
>   So often seen the resurrection morn,
>   I go triumphant, though new Calvaries wait."

And this freedom and victory are waiting only for those lives that have been broken beneath the cross of an absolute restraint of God, and have so mastered themselves under God's name by the help of Christ that control has been given over in trust into their own hands.

And we all know that power is to be won here in this school where men are trained both to feel and to wield dominion. There is no power in the world that is not power cabined, power held in some way. Loose power is imperceptible and utterly useless. The only power we know is power walled in, shut down, confined and beating against its barriers and its walls. We know this in the athletic life of our colleges to-day. No athletic trainer in any college ever followed David's method with Adonijah. The trainer is there to say: "Why did you do it that way?" "Why did you not do it this way? You have no right to waste your energy in that way. You must do it so." There is one scene in *Quo Vadis* that redeems much else in the book. It is the scene in the Coliseum, when the giant Gothic slave is shown saving the life of his mistress, whom he loved. The great bull has come out with the girl's form tied to his horns, and there is dead silence as the bull stands angrily facing the man. You remember the picture. As Ursus lays one hand on each horn of the auroch the struggle begins. There is not a sound. The great multitude watches the man's muscles rise and harden and the sweat come out and drop from every pore. They see his feet sinking down in the arena, until the sand is above his ankles. Suddenly the great head of the bull begins to twist under that awful strength. Then the neck breaks and the giant lifts the limp form from the beast's neck and stands with the burden in his hands before the Emperor. One likes to read such a picture of power secured by self-discipline. Do we want to go out limp and beaten and ineffective in our lives against the great mass of work in the world that waits to be done? Or do we want to go in the strength of Him Who, having bent beneath His Father's will, was able to carry on the Cross the whole burden of human sin?

And we must learn in this school the things we value and desire most: purity and delicacy and refinement of character, for they cannot be acquired elsewhere. So much social standing nowadays is uttered in terms of self-assertion and indulgence and the ability to have any whim or caprice gratified. This sort of self-assertion, this caprice, is regarded by many of us as the highest mark of social authority, whereas we know it is precisely the opposite, that it is self-restraint and self-control and self-surrender that mark the finest lives.

There is a beautiful story in the life of Goldwin Smith that illustrates what I mean. In the early sixties, when he was one of the keenest liberal minds of England, he was associated with Cobden and Bright in the Manchester School. Again and again he found himself the mark of the bitterest criticism from Disraeli. Later Goldwin Smith, resigning his professorship at Oxford, came to Canada. At that time Disraeli's novel, "Lothair," appeared in which he attacked Smith—of course, without using his name—as a social parasite. It stung Smith to the depths of his soul, but as it was an anonymous book there was nothing he could do but sit down and write this note personally to Disraeli :

"You well know that if you had ventured openly to accuse me of any social baseness, you would have had to answer for your words ; but when sheltering yourself under the literary forms of a work of fiction, you seek to traduce with impunity the social character of a political opponent, your expressions can touch no man's honour—they are the stingless insults of a coward."

That was all he did. And yet, at that very moment, Goldwin Smith had in his possession letters of Disraeli, with which he could have crushed him. Openly in Parliament Disraeli had said that he had never asked Peel for any position. But among Peel's papers which had been placed in his hands Smith had a letter in which Disraeli had abjectly begged Peel to give him office. All that Smith needed to do was to publish Disraeli's own letter to Peel and it would have ruined Disraeli's career. But to Goldwin Smith that was not a noble thing to do. Peel's correspondence had not been given to him to use in self-defense, or for any personal justification of his own, and he repressed that letter until Disraeli was dead. Then, years after, all of Peel's correspondence was published and the whole world knew what a gentleman Goldwin Smith had been. Our modern ideals of what constitutes high social and national standing and character say: "Fight fire with fire. Dishonour releases honour from itself. He struck you foul; strike him so in return." But the man who had learned self-restraint in the school of God's loyalty and truth, who understood that power is ours, not to use for self-seeking, but for the good of men and for God's honour, would not stoop to any such disloyalty and shame.

Once more. Whose judgment is of any value? Who would have thought of going to Adonijah and asking his opinion on anything whatsoever? He did not know right from wrong. He never thought over the issues of right or wrong. What would I like to do? What does passion bid me do? What is my whim or caprice for to-night?—that was as far as Adonijah had ever thought. No man would ever go to him, as no men will ever come to you and me if we have not been trained in the school of moral discrimination, if we have not looked on ethical principle and duty in deciding the question whether each thing is really right for us and for the whole world. If we are to be men and women to whom people will come for comfort and strength and guidance, to whom our own children can come with assurance that they will get the truth, we must be men and women who now place ourselves beneath the firm discipline of God.

We see all this put simply in two great things. We see it in our Lord's constant appeal, while here in the world, for men and women of fiber and discipline. One came to Him and said: "Lord, what shall I do to inherit eternal life?" And Jesus, looking upon him, loved him and said: "I would not think of counselling anything hard. You must not sacrifice anything. It is all very easy. The Father above is a Father of great tenderness and compassion. He would not lay a straw's weight upon any child of His. Go; live according to your desires and by the natural impulses of your heart, and for that you shall have treasure in heaven." Oh, no; He did not say that. He said: "Go, sell all that thou hast, and come and follow me. Except ye love less than duty your father and mother and brother and sister, yea, and your own life also, ye cannot enter the kingdom of God."

We see it, too, in God's way with men as He laid down His great laws at the beginning, when His people were but as a race of little children.

Why did He not say to them : " This ye may do. The world is sweet and fair. This ye may do, and all shall be easy to you"? Why, on the other hand, did He speak to them in the stern admonitions of the Decalogue : " Thou shalt. Thou shalt not"? God never hesitates to lay His great denials upon mankind and at last to stifle us beneath the restraint of death that He may issue us forth through that restraint into the infinite liberties of the life immortal.

Now do not brush all this away to-day, or any day, light-heartedly, as it can be so easily brushed away. " Oh, don't shadow our lives," you will say, " with your denials and your prohibitions and your restraints. Leave life free and sweet as the summer air and the flowers of the field "— that last how long? No, my friends, it were well for us that we should learn this lesson, and learn it now, ere the time comes when the silver cord is loosed and the wheel is broken at the cistern and the grinders cease and the long shadows fall. You remember a tragic incident in New York a few years ago—I do not need to recall the details of it—when two young lives made shipwreck of themselves just because they thought that im-pulse and caprice were the free voices that they might obey. When it was all over, and the two lives had drawn the veil of night across their short-lived evil joy, one of the papers published a letter which the girl had written to a friend :

"My friend," she wrote, "you and I and Fred, young, heedless, cynical, living in this reckless town of New York, may laugh sometimes at the old things like law and religion, when they say, 'Thou shalt not.' We may think that phrase was written for old fogies, and we may sneer at 'the wages of sin is death'; but, my friend, there comes to us some time knowledge that the law and religion are right. What they say we shall not do, we cannot do without suffering. Fred and I have learned that. The wages of sin is death."

It is worse than death; for what was Hell in that great vision that John saw? Why, nothing but the removal of all restraint. "He which is filthy, let him be filthy still." He is unclean, let him be unclean. He is unholy, let him be unholy. Take all the restraints away. That is Hell.

Away from the dark gates that open thither may another voice call us here to-day, the clear, strong, summoning voice of Him Who said of Himself: "I came not to do mine own will, but the will of him that sent me. I do always those things that please my Father," and Who in the garden of Gethsemane, when the anguish was almost greater than He could bear, yet found rest when He prayed, "Father, not my will, but thine be done"; that out of the willfulness and capriciousness and the whim and mood of our little self-indulgent lives we may pass into the great, strong, steadfast, sovereign will that waits for us;

that we may stand fast and be strong in the strength and chastening of God!

Now I have put it—this matter of our need of discipline—in the most personal and individual way, but it is our great national and corporate need. The body of a nation can only exist through the ordered discipline of its members and the spirit of a nation like the spirit of a man needs to be cleansed of all the lusts of willfulness and self-indulgence. The spirit of our American nation needs such cleansing. Mr. Kipling has drawn us his picture of it:

" Through many roads, by me possessed,
    He shambles forth in cosmic guise;
He is the Jester and the Jest,
    And he the Text himself applies.

" His easy unswept hearth he lends
    From Labrador to Guadaloupe;
Till, elbowed out by sloven friends,
    He camps, at sufferance, on the stoop.

" Calm-eyed he scoffs at sword and crown,
    Or panic-blinded stabs and slays:
Blatant he bids the world bow down,
    Or cringing begs a crust of praise;

" Or, sombre-drunk, at mine and mart,
    He dubs his dreary brethren Kings.
His hands are black with blood—his heart
    Leaps, as a babe's, at little things.

" But, through the shift of mood and mood,
    Mine ancient humour saves him whole —
The cynic devil in his blood
    That bids him mock his hurrying soul;

" That bids him flout the Law he makes,
　　That bids him make the Law he flouts,
Till, dazed by many doubts, he wakes
　　The drumming guns that—have no doubts ;

" That checks him foolish-hot and fond,
　　That chuckles through his deepest ire,
That gilds the slough of his despond
　　But dims the goal of his desire ;

" Inopportune, shrill-accented,
　　The acrid Asiatic mirth
That leaves him, careless 'mid his dead,
　　The scandal of the elder earth."

Doubtless we do not like this picture. We call it a libel or a caricature. Let it be so. Draw your own picture. If there is any truth or faithfulness in it, if it is not blind with national vanity and self-deceit, it will still be a revelation of national need of discipline and of self-empire.

And how can such discipline and self-empire be won ? Well, it will not be won on any ground of prudential expediency or practical self-interest. It is well for men and nations to discern their moral shortcomings and to realize their need of a new character. But there are no automatic processes of community salvation. The disciplined nation comes in only one way—by the answers of individuals to the austere call of the one Person who can remake character and mould the stuff of manhood and nationality. The austere call! This is the nation's need and it is the fundamental summons and the central note

of Christianity. "Then said Jesus unto his disciples, If any man will come after me, let him
deny himself, and take up his cross, and follow
me."

The appeal of Christ was always addressed to
the sacrificial and the heroic. In every call
which He issued to men there is this unmistakable note of austerity. He never smooths
things over for the sake of pleasing people or of
winning followers. There were times when He
seemed almost needlessly to draw in these repelling aspects of discipleship, and to make the
conditions of following Him unnecessarily hard.
It is related that it came to pass that, as they
went in the way, a certain man said unto Him,
"Lord, I will follow thee whithersoever thou
goest." And Jesus said unto him, "Foxes have
holes, and birds of the air have nests; but the
Son of man hath not where to lay his head."
And He said unto another, "Follow me." But
he said, "Lord, suffer me first to go and bury
my father." Jesus said unto him, "Let the dead
bury their dead; but go thou and preach the
kingdom of God." And another also said,
"Lord, I will follow thee; but let me first go bid
them farewell which are at home at my house."
And Jesus said unto him, "No man, having put
his hand to the plough, and looking back, is fit
for the kingdom of God."

Christ never concealed His own judgments

and convictions as to life's values in these matters, and spoke with the greatest scorn of all indulgence and softness of life. "What went ye out for to see?" He asked the people, regarding John. "A man clothed in soft raiment? Behold, they that wear soft clothing are in king's houses." He was looking after men of iron and of austerity. "If any man will come after me, let him deny himself, and take up his cross and follow me."

The beautiful thing is that this appeal of Christ's was not futile. Instead of repelling men it drew them. He actually obtained the men whom He was hunting for, not by offering them worldly inducements, not by making such appeals as anybody but Christ would have made, but by addressing the sacrificial spirit in them, and making an appeal to their latent capacity for heroism. There is a wonderful tribute in Jesus' method to those characteristics in human nature which have never been destroyed, which can answer to the highest motives, which do not need to be bought by any low compensations, but which spring into full life when appealed to on the most heroic and unselfish plane. We know how, in consequence, this exultation in difficulties, this love of hardship, this scorn of ease became the characteristic note of early Christianity. In the best summary description which Saint Paul gives of Christian character and manhood, in the twelfth chapter of Romans we find him speaking of "rejoicing in hope; patient in tribulation." And when he comes to write his conception of the character of the happy warrior, we find him setting this in the foreground, "Endure hardship, as a good soldier of Jesus Christ." The praise of the New Testament is never given to those who have lived in luxurious, indulgent ease. It is for that little company of men and women who have loved the difficult tasks, and who with joy trod the rough ways that transcend the stars. Every one of the great New Testament leaders is a man who exalts for us this same love of moral hardship, this same scorn of indulgence and smooth ease, and this same virtue of steadfastness, "And not only so," says Paul, "but we glory in tribulations also: knowing that tribulation worketh stedfastness; and stedfastness, experience; and experience, hope." And Peter writes, "Yea, and for this very cause adding on your part all diligence, in your faith supply virtue; and in your virtue knowledge; and in your knowledge self-control; and in your self-control stedfastness; and in your stedfastness godliness." James joins in, "My brethren, count it all joy when ye fall into divers temptations; knowing this, that the trying of your faith worketh patience." And you remember the description which John gives of himself in Revelation as "your brother and partaker with you in the tribulation and kingdom and stedfastness which are in Jesus."

Now, we ask ourselves the question why our Lord poured out all this scorn on what the world counts the desirable condition and atmosphere of life, why the New Testament has no patience with self-seeking, indulgence, contentment, or ease as the standard of a human life, why it speaks contemptuously of smooth ease of every kind, and exalts, instead, the austere life, the life of strength, and of self-discipline, why our Lord said to men when He came to call them into the best thing there was in the world, "If any man will come after me, let him deny himself, and take up his cross daily, and follow after me."

Well, one reason why the whole New Testament pours out such contempt upon the smooth life and exalts hardness, is because only hardness can make a great soul, and the end of the Gospel, the end of life, was the growing of souls. The words of Socrates, understood in the social sense which he intended and not selfishly, contain the central end. "For I do nothing," said he, "but go about persuading you all, old and young alike, not to take thought for your persons or your properties, but first and chiefly to care about the greatest improvement of the soul." It is true, in a sense, that we are here for the work we can do, but it is also true, in a yet deeper sense, that we are here to become the best workmen that we can become, and that the work we do has a large measure of its value in its reflex power of making us capable of doing better work.   Evidently this is not the real workshop where God needs His best men and women. When He has perfected His workmen and workwomen and recognizes that they are prepared to do their best work, does He make use of them here?   Never.   He takes them elsewhere, where evidently the real work is to be done.   Everything we see in this world would seem to indicate that it is only the preparatory school, a place where men and women are equipped for the real thing, that the career that is to abide lies elsewhere than here.   The purpose of these days is to make us ready for the work God has for us to do in a larger sphere than this, where we pass on, as Chinese Gordon told Mr. Huxley, to have a larger government given to us to administer. God pours out His contempt on smoothness of life because it cannot make greatness of soul, and greatness of soul is one object of our being here.

The Christian ideal despised, also, this smoothness which seems to many of us the most desirable thing that life has for us, because there is such little knowledge given with it.   At best it can only play on the very surface of life.   We know no more than springs out of the deep experience through which we pass. You remember the lines of Father Tabb :

> " ' Where wast thou, little song,
> That hast delayed so long
> To come to me ? '
> ' Mute in the mind of God
> Till where thy feet had trod
> I followed thee.' "

It is only where we have gone that we know the way ; it is only the experience in life that we have passed through that gives us our true knowledge of life, because the end of life is its relationships, and wealth of life depends on the breadth of true knowledge and the riches of true relationship. Smoothness of life is simply deadening because it keeps us out of what is real life.

And Christianity derided smoothness of life, and scorned it, because it separates us from fellowship with the noble and suffering life of God. You know the long controversy in theology as to whether the idea of suffering is compatible with the idea of a perfect God. There have been some theologians who insist it could not be possible that God should suffer. If He could suffer, He could not be God. Well, I suppose all of us here are prepared without one moment of hesitation to range ourselves on the other side, and to say that if God cannot suffer He cannot be our God. He could not be a father if He did not suffer. Christ could not have been the revelation of Him if He is not a suffering God; for "He was the man of sorrows, and acquainted with grief." What He laid bare was a heart of love sharing the anguish of others; for we have not a Father who cannot be touched with the feeling of our infirmities,—We can say that of Him because of what we know of Him who revealed Him,—We have not a Father who cannot be touched with the feeling of our infirmities, no impassive God sitting where "no sound of human sorrow mounts to mar His sacred everlasting calm," but a Father who pities His children, who enters into their life, and who loves them with all His soul. We can have no knowledge of that God, no fellowship with His life, if what we are living is the smooth, easy, indulgent life, everything bought for us by others, nothing done by us for others, no blood of sacrifice colouring our life red with the glow of God and His incarnate Son. The New Testament despises the smooth life that makes it impossible for men and women to have any part in the deepest life of their Father.

And the New Testament scorns the smooth, indulgent life because it cannot connect men and women with the real springs of strength and of power. No strong man was ever made against no resistance. We develop no physical power by putting forth no physical effort. All the strength of life we have we get by pushing against opposition. We acquire power as we draw it out of deep experience and effort. And the new Christian ideal made no place for indulgence and ease because these things leave men and women weak, with no strength either themselves to bear or to achieve for others. It is as Mrs. King puts it in Ugo Bassi's "Sermon in the Hospital" :

" The Vine from every living limb bleeds wine ;
  Is it the poorer for the spirit shed ?
  The drunkard and the wanton drink thereof ;
  Are they the richer for that gift's excess ?
  Measure thy life by loss instead of gain ;
  Not by the wine drunk, but the wine poured forth
  For love's strength standeth in love's sacrifice ;
  And whoso suffers most hath most to give.

  .   .   .   .   .   .

      God said to Man and Woman, ' By thy sweat,
  And by thy travail, thou shalt conquer earth,'
  Not, by thy ease or pleasure : —and no good
  Or glory of this life but comes by pain.
  How poor were earth if all its martrydoms,
  If all its struggling sighs of sacrifice
  Were swept away, and all were satiate-smooth,
  If this were such a heaven of soul and sense
  As some have dreamed of ;—and we human still.
  Nay, we were fashioned not for perfect peace
  In this world, howsoever in the next :
  And what we win and hold is through some strife."

And it was because our Lord knew this that He set over against men's wills the strait door of the kingdom of life. He did not betray the trust that had been given to Him. He did not say,

"Come, I will make life easy for you." He did not say, "Come, let us indulge ourselves to heart's content." He said, "If any man will come after me, let him leave all that behind, let him deny himself, and let him take up his cross daily, and let him come after me."

Now, I know what many of us will be saying of all this. We will be saying, "God did not bring us into the world with any cross. All our life long has been a sheltered life. None of this hardness of which you speak has ever come to us. Maybe our fathers and mothers knew it before us, but they have shielded us from its pressure. Are we to go back to crudeness and asceticism for the good of our souls? Are we who have no cross deliberately to take our smooth lives and roughen them?" Yes, that is precisely what I am saying. Those of us who were not born with a cross must find one, those whose lives have been smooth are deliberately to find ways of roughening them, so that we may know a life of power and fellowship with the suffering God, and can go out to real work, and be prepared for that greater life and greater service which await us elsewhere than here.

We shall not have any great difficulty in obeying this call of Christ to roughen our lives. There are many crosses in the world too heavy for the men and women who are trying to carry them. We can go out and find one of these

crosses and help to bear it. They are not far
away. Here is a clipping from the New York
Sun :

"A comely young Hungarian woman with a three-
months-old baby in her arms dropped to the sidewalk at
Fifth Avenue and Fourteenth Street late yesterday afternoon and lay half conscious. An ambulance surgeon who
came said the woman was starving and that her baby had
bronchitis.

"The woman recovered enough to tell the surgeon that
she was Mrs. Mary Scheinn, twenty years old, and that her
husband had died recently. She had been living with a
friend at 97 Seigel Street, Brooklyn, she said, but this
woman also was very poor and expected to be evicted to-
day, so Mrs. Scheinn had walked to New York to try to
get her sick child into a hospital. She tramped from
hospital to hospital, and everywhere they refused to take
the child, she said. But she kept up the quest until she
gave out. She had had nothing to eat since yesterday and
little then.

"The ambulance took the woman and child to Bellevue
Hospital. Both are in a rather serious condition."

Being young and comely, doubtless, if she had
not had the baby, some pimp or other American
citizen, for a consideration within her power,
might have helped her, but being innocent and
carrying a baby there she stood until she fell
down, on the corner of Fifth Avenue and Fourteenth Street, in the heart of the city, a woman
carrying a baby and a cross that were too heavy
for her. There were millions of Christian people

round about her.   Thousands of us never knew
what a cross was and we let the woman with her
child in her arms fall down under the weight of
hers.   This world is black with the shadows of
crosses.   If we have none of our own, in the
name of the great Cross, let us borrow one.

Here is a note from a girl.   She is one of
thousands and the note is real.   I had been
speaking in one of the New York churches and
the next day came a letter from her asking me,
if I really believed what I had said, to answer
some questions for her.   I wrote in reply and
this was part of her answer: " The great trouble
with me is that I have to fight continually
against despondency.   Life to me is a series of
sorrows and troubles, that accumulate and grow
larger, and just when I am at the point of giving
up altogether some little word or act deters me.
. . .   I know I would be happy if I were, as you
say, truly trustful towards God, but God to me
seems very far off and rather mythical.   Your letter, also the fact that you wrote, was a help to me.
The part that perhaps appealed to me most was
the idea that God and God's love are longing
for us.   It is very fine to feel that when one is
always lonesome."   I learned more of her story
but it is not for telling here.   It was a cross too
heavy for her which she was trying to bear.
Women who knew her lifted its weight for her,
taking it over upon themselves.

And not only by taking up crosses, of which the world is full, can we roughen our lives. Many of us can do it by simply cutting off some of our waste and extravagance.   There are many of us who never ask before we spend money, " How can I get the greatest return from this money ? " We waste it like water, while Belgium, Serbia, Poland and Armenia call. It is said that there are thirty million people in India who have only one meal a day, and who never know what it is to have enough to eat. Some of them say that if they could have enough to eat for just two days, they would be willing to lie down and die content. Again and again, hundreds of thousands of people in China have been the victims of famine, while we were throwing wealth away. We can roughen life a bit by denying ourselves, by abridging expenditure and devoting the money to human need and to some of the services the world is dying for.

Students often reject the ethical and economic arguments against gambling. These arguments are valid but it is very hard to get a clutch for them on many minds. You can point out how dishonourable and essentially immoral it is for a man to have money which he did not earn, for which he gave no equivalent, which came to him as no expression of friendship or by no legitimate inheritance. All this is clear to the healthy and manly moral sense. But the gambler

does not have such a sense. I have often wondered that the case is not more frequently put
from the other side, from the side of the wrong
of spending money in gambling. When a man
has won on a bet the moral question is lulled
but when he has lost there is a chastened mood
which can be invited to reflect. What moral
warrant did he have for throwing his money
away? What does he have to show for it?
A million hungry hands were outstretched to
him, a world of want and suffering called
towards him over land and sea? And he threw
his money away—got nothing for it, did nothing
with it. In a world like ours, there are parched
lips waiting for drink; there are hungry mouths
in need of bread :—do we have any right to waste
in indulgence in a world like this? Men should
scrutinize every dollar that passes through their
hands and ask, "What is the very best thing
that I can do with this?"

And frugality, self-imposed for the sake of
service, will come back to us in rich reward in
character and power. Horace Bushnell drew a
noble picture of the fruitage of true parsimony
in his address at the Litchfield County Centennial
in 1851, on "The Age of Homespun":

"It was also a great point, in this homespun
mode of life, that it imparted exactly what many
speak of only with contempt, a closely girded
habit of economy. Harnessed, all together, into

the producing process, young and old, male and female, from the boy that rode the plow-horse, to the grandmother knitting under her spectacles, they had no conception of squandering lightly what they all had been at work, thread by thread, and grain by grain, to produce. They knew too exactly what everything cost, even small things, not to husband them carefully. Men of patrimony in the great world, therefore, noticing their small way in trade, or expenditure, are ready, as we often see, to charge them with meanness—simply because they knew things only in the small; or, what is not far different, because they were too simple and rustic to have any conception of the big operations by which other men are wont to get their money without earning it, and lavish the more freely because it was not earned. Still, this knowing life only in the small, it will be found, is really anything but meanness.

"Probably enough the man who is heard threshing in his barn of a winter evening, by the light of a lantern, (I knew such an example) will be seen driving his team next day, the coldest day of the year, through the deep snow to a distant wood-lot to draw a load for a present to his minister. So the housewife that higgles for a half hour with the merchant over some small trade is yet one that will keep watch, not unlikely, when the schoolmaster, boarding round the district, comes to some hard quarter, and commence asking him to dinner, then to tea, then to stay over night, and literally boarding him, till the hard quarter is passed. Who now, in the great world of money, will do, not to say the same, as much, proportionally as much, in any of the pure hospitalities of life ?

" Besides, what sufficiently disproves any real meanness, it will be found that children brought up, in this way, to know things in the small— what they cost and what is their value—have, in just that fact, one of the best securities of character and most certain elements of power and success in life ; because they expect to get on by small advances followed up and saved by others, not by sudden leaps of fortune that despise the slow but surer methods of industry and merit. When the hard, wiry-looking patriarch of homespun, for example, sets off for Hartford, or Bridgeport, to exchange the little surplus of his year's production, carrying his provision with him and the fodder for his team, and taking his boy along to show him the great world, you may laugh at the simplicity, or pity, if you will, the sordid look of the picture ; but, five or ten years hence, this boy will probably enough be found in college, digging out the cent's worths of his father's money in hard study ; and some twenty years later he will be returning, in his honours, as the celebrated Judge, or Governor, or Senator and

public orator, from some one of the great states
of the republic, to bless the sight once more of
that venerated pair who shaped his beginnings,
and planted the small seeds of his future success.
Small seeds, you may have thought, of meanness; but now they have grown up and blos-
somed into a large-minded life, a generous public
devotion, and a free benevolence to mankind.

"And just here, I am persuaded, is the secret,
in no small degree, of the very peculiar success
that has distinguished the sons of Connecticut,
and, not least, those of Litchfield County, in
their migration to other states. It is because
they have gone out in the wise economy of a
simple, homespun training, expecting to get on
in the world by merit and patience, and by a
careful husbanding of small advances; secured
in their virtue by just that which makes their
perseverance successful. For the men who see
the great in the small, and go on to build the
great by small increments, and so form a character of integrity before God and men, as solid
and massive as the outward successes they conquer. The great men who think to be great in
general, having yet nothing great in particular,
are a much more windy affair."

Every one ought to roughen life by friendships
that will bring into it those influences which are
not naturally in our daily associations and will
carry us into contact with men and women who

struggle harder than we do.   A few such friendships will help to keep life from petrification and
to make us aware that the world is under a cross,
and that our hearts must be as open to all its
needs as the heart of the Father of human life is
open always.

And we can help to roughen our lives in the
very sense in which Christ meant them to be
roughened if we will resist the steadily increasing
tendency of our day to multiply ways in which
we are released from doing things for ourselves.
There are none of us who do not have a hundred
things done for us that our fathers and mothers
had to do for themselves.   Little by little, we are
ridding ourselves of the responsibility of doing
any service for ourselves whatsoever.   There is
immense gain in this.   It gives freedom for larger
living but it can go too far, and it would be a
great thing if we resolved at periods that we
would not let anybody else do for us what we
could do for ourselves.   There was a day, perhaps, when men needed the other rule, when it
was a great deal better to get other people to do
things for us than to do them ourselves, but the
time has come when the world needs to reverse
that principle.   What the world wants is not
organizers, but deorganizers, men and women
who will increase the number of personal services
and activities, and who will bring something
frugal, simple and elementary back into life to

deliver us from the false heaven of ease and self-indulgence, which is as bad as any other kind of hell.   Christ came to save us from that.

There is one other way in which we can answer this call, and can deliver ourselves from the curse of smooth living.   Around about us on every side there are causes waiting for what men and women can do for them.   I do not mean crosses in any great, general, organized sense, in which we send our five, our twenty-five or our hundred dollars to some society and think we have, in that way, carried all the cross that Christ means to have us carry.   We cannot fulfill Christ's command by paying an organization to carry a cross for us.   All the work they do must be done, and it must be supported.   Millions of dollars that are not being given now ought to be given. But what Christ is waiting for also and what we have got to do if we are to have the satisfaction of the enduring life is to find each of us for himself some true cross of personal service.   There are men and women around us who are waiting for some touch of sympathy, some kindness, some unflinching word of ours to them that shall mean the awakening of their own discouraged or sleeping souls, that they may come out to live. "If any man will come after me, let him deny himself, and take up his cross and follow me."

One of the saddest things in the world to-day is the principle under which those are living who are unwilling to bear these crosses and to bring home into their lives the wholesome spiritual stimulus that this roughening of life alone can give to them. We have reacted too far from the old monastic idea. Men speak with scorn now of those men and women who went away into monasteries and convents, despising the joys of the world for the sake of their souls. But these men and women were infinitely better than the great multitudes who go out into the world to-day, despising their souls for the sake of the joys of the world. If a man or woman wants to do any despising it is better to despise the world than the soul. It were well for us to go back a little to the spirit of the mediæval time. When that spirit was pure and good the world's richest service flowed out from it.

The glory of life for us consists in finding the rough, the morally austere things in life and then fearlessly and unhesitatingly doing them. There is no splendour in the easy indulgent way. The splendour lies in finding the hard thing to be achieved and revelling in it.

Many years ago I clipped this story from the editorials of what was then our ablest newspaper :

" A young Briton named Felix Oswald became interested a while ago in the geology of Turkish Armenia. He made long journeys through that country and finally came home with an important amount of valuable new material. It was not matter, however, that would find favour in the eyes of the general publisher and Mr. Oswald had to undertake its publication himself. He had the type set at the lowest rates in a small town. There were 516 pages of print and the author undertook the large task of doing the printing himself. He hired a hand press and after weeks of hard work he had produced 101 copies of the book. Feeling certain that this edition would fill the demand he went about the next large job, which was the hand colouring of all his maps and profiles. Then the copies were bound and the book was out.

" Leading geologists say that the work is one of the best of its kind. The small edition is exhausted and the book will not be reprinted. The editor of *Petermann's Mitteilungen*, believing that a wide circle of geologists would be glad to have the important results of Oswald's investigations, has just printed in his periodical an extended résumé of them together with some of the maps. The University of London has crowned the work with its approval by conferring the degree of Doctor of Science upon the author. Oswald has certainly earned the congratulations of all who admire the qualities of courage, perseverance and intelligent devotion to a special task."

A man does not have to go to Armenia to find

the hard thing to do, although there are harder and nobler tasks waiting there to-day than Oswald undertook, tasks that are crosses in the divinest sense, scarred with sorrow and grief. And perhaps there are some among us here now who are bearing crosses and finding them beyond their strength. But they are not to be mourned over. They were not of our making, were they? If they were of our making, perhaps there is some penitence to be felt, some restitution to be made. If they were not of our making, we may be sure that they were built just for our shoulder, that One who knew us made them that we might carry them, and become under them what we could never become without them. And if we have no such cross, out from our smooth and easy living, our cozy shelters in which we have been kept and are kept now, One is calling us to come whose ancient word we hear to-day: "I came not to send peace, but a sword. Whosoever would be my disciple must love nothing as much as me, and must be willing to rise up and follow me." For men and women who will do this in the full and joyous spirit of Francis of Assisi but in the forms suitable to our modern life the summons of God and the world is clear.

LECTURE II

THE CONSERVATION AND RELEASE OF MORAL RESOURCES

ONE of our most familiar national ideas during recent years has been the conservation of our natural resources, our mines, our forests, our water power, the agricultural capacities of our soil. It would have been a good thing if this idea had occurred to us fifty years earlier. But it is an idea which always comes late to a young nation. So long as the population is sparse and the supply of good land unlimited and it is an easy thing to pick up a living from the surface of the ground, perhaps it is too much to expect that any people would be careful and frugal. But when the population has increased and begins to press against the means of subsistence, when the good public lands are exhausted and a mere living becomes harder for the masses of the people to secure, then any nation awakens to wisdom and turns from recklessness and prodigality.

And, doubtless, the idea would have occurred to us a full generation earlier if it had not been for the terrible education of our Civil War. There is a great deal to be set down on the

good side of the account of the Civil War. It took the putty of our national character and burned it into stone. It ran steel fibres through our national life. And it brought us for the first time to a sense of national unity. But alas there is a great deal also on the ledger's other page. For war is not conservation, it is destruction. It educates any people not in frugality but in wastefulness. Military supplies must be bought at once at any cost. Everything is thrown away with a negligent and wasteful hand. And so long as any people is pouring out its best possession, the precious life-blood of its sons, like water on the battle-field, you cannot expect it to be saving and careful in its material possessions.

The days of waste that followed the Civil War are gone forever. The nation has begun now to count carefully the amount of its available wealth. We have seen calculations of how many millions of feet of lumber we have standing in our forests and how many millions of tons of coal we have still hid away in our treasure houses underground. And far and wide over the nation now we are learning to husband the resources we have left, mindful of our children who are to come after us.

And it is a good thing that the nation in conserving her resources realizes that there is something more important than a careful husbanding of her mere material wealth. The vital resources

of any people are of more significance to her
than clods of coal, or timber on her hillsides.
Of what use would it be to conserve the material
resources of any nation if we conserve them only
for a deteriorating racial stock?   The nation has
come to realize that the men and women who
compose it are its largest wealth, and that this
treasure must be guarded more sacredly than
our mines, our forests, or our water power.   We
have seen, accordingly, a whole new body of
legislation growing up, that would have made
our fathers stand aghast, fixing the conditions of
employment, the age of employees, the sanitary
condition of homes and mills, the hours of work
and the care of women.   The expenditure of immense sums for the protection of the life and
health of factory labourers is now readily recognized even by "soul-less corporations," which
formerly fought against all such outlay, as money
well invested.   In all the nation to-day we
realize that there is a more precious wealth than
our material wealth.   I saw an interesting illustration of this new frame of mind a little while
ago in a statement issued by some leading men
in Tennessee dealing with the excessive death
rate among the negroes of the South.   They
pointed out that among nine millions of white
people the death rate is 160,000, and that among
the nine millions of the negroes the death rate is
266,000.   In other words, among the negroes,

106,000 more people die every year than among a corresponding number of the whites of our country. In the negro, these men argued, the South had an invaluable asset, a better type of labour on the whole, with all its drawbacks, than any other section of the nation possessed, more docile, more faithful, less troublesome, and the South could not afford to lose this labour which it needed for developing its wealth. These men estimated the economic value of each one of these lives at $350 a year, and the period of that economic value at ten years, so that each one of these wasted lives was a loss of $3,500 to the South, or $371,000,000 each year, one million dollars a day, and they argued that the South could not afford such a waste. The South, they held, must see that the death rate among the negro is reduced to the same proportions as the death rate among the white people, in order that such an enormous economic loss might be averted. We are realizing all over the nation now that a man is a very costly product. You can breed an animal in a few months for the market, but it takes twenty years to grow a man, and no nation can afford to throw away such costly products as men and women. These are its most priceless wealth. If it expects to conserve its treasures and to be prepared for the services of the days to come, it is bound to guard this wealth more sacredly than any other. And American capital and industry have come to see this clearly. Here is one typical utterance by a leading engineer at a meeting of the Immigration Committee of the Chamber of Commerce of the United States :

"Industrial Americanization is a part of the prevalent present-day movement towards the humanizing of industry. It aims to make what is commonly called 'welfare work' not an exercise of the individual employer's 'paternalism,' but a legitimate kind of business organization everywhere. There are now innumerable kinds of 'welfare work.' One employer does it from the point of view of 'good business'; another on the 'big brothers' theory. One man confines himself to playgrounds, another to safety appliances. In one firm it is under the employment manager; in another under a Y. M. C. A. director; and in a number of other firms it is classified in as many different ways.

"There is no agreement among American employers as to where the organization of the human side of industry really belongs. And there are absolutely no standards for it. What we need to do is to extend scientific methods to the human phases of industrial organization, and thus give 'welfare work' a definite place and definite standards. The engineer as the 'consulting mind' of industry must be the leader in this work. It is he who determines the site of the plant and its construction. Inside the plant again, the engineer has much to do with efficiency methods. No efficiency methods that are unrelated to the men in the plant can prosper permanently."

But there is another sort of resource and national treasure greater by far than these, which

most of the nations are passing by. I mean the latent and undeveloped capacities for ministry and achievement which lie dormant inside human life. Every life is a reservoir of unawakened possibilities. There is no one of us that is more than a fraction of the man he should be. There is not one who is not falling short by a wide margin of the ideals that he ought to attain, not one who is making the contribution to the nation or building the share in the Kingdom of God that God and mankind alike have a right to expect of him. Not long before his death, an article contributed by Prof. William James, of Harvard, appeared in the *American Magazine*, entitled "The Powers of Man," in which Professor James argued that mankind is living on a very small fraction of its vitality, and that there are buried underground strata of possibilities and of power which are never tapped except in times of great emergency. For a little time then a man draws on these reserves, and then seals the strata over again and falls back on the surface levels once more. For illustration he spoke of the familiar phenomenon of the second wind. Every boy can remember such experiences. There came a time in the game when he was "all in." He had done his best and drawn on his last available power. Suddenly it was as though something broke. A partition wall fell in. Unsuspected reserves were released. The second wind came and reservoirs of power that had been withheld came unexpectedly into play and he did better than he had done before, what he had never been able to do before. That is an absolute truth of experience all through life. In our great crises, any one of many forces may unlock these energies and let them loose. And the present needed appeal of the world is to men and women that they should not be content to draw upon these reservoirs in crises alone. The tragic crises come because these powers are not drawn forth and used. The great wealth of the nations and of the world that needs now to be unsealed is just this wealth of moral capacity lying latent and dormant within.

What I have been saying is certainly true in the realm of our physical energies. I remember a story of John Lawrence, who went out to India a raw, uninfluential Irish boy in the service of the East India Company, resolved to do his work well and make himself a name. Very early in his career he was assigned to the collectorship of the Jullundur Doab, on what was then the frontier of India. He made himself perfectly at home among his people, entering into their life, mastering their vernaculars, learning their secrets, until at last men came to think of "Jans Larens" as a demi-god with powers beyond the knowledge of common men. One day as he was sitting in his house a messenger came in from one of his

districts and reported that a village was burning down and begged him to come. He hurried out to the village. When he arrived he asked the headmen if they had all the people out of the houses and was told that all had been brought out except one old woman who refused to come. He went to the house where the woman lived and looked in. There she sat on a bag of grain. Lawrence entreated her to come out but she refused, explaining that this bag of grain was all her earthly wealth. If she came out she would starve; she would rather stay and be burned. When Lawrence found his commands and entreaties unavailing, he rushed in, with the embers from the burning roof falling on his shoulders, stooped over and picked up the bag of grain, and left the burning building, the old woman following obediently behind. The next day as he was sitting in his house it flashed on his mind that the bag of grain had been exceedingly heavy and he rode out curiously to the village again to see how much he had lifted. He had no difficulty in finding the old woman and her bag of grain. He stooped over to lift it but could not budge it from the ground. But the day before he had budged it. He had picked it up and carried it. The power to do it was lying latent in him all the while. All he needed was just the piercing call or inspiration adequate to release the buried energy.

And the world is full of evidences that what is true physically is true morally. In every man lies the power with the grace and help of God to meet his great crisis and in every woman the power to bear the agony and pain of her great hour. Only a few years ago, when the *Titanic* went down and some men who had walked as dogs at the heel of their passions suddenly became masters of themselves and laughing stood at attention to death as they waited on the deck, we all wondered what it was that gave these men who had been slaves their sudden moral mastery. That mastery was within all the time. It did not come out of the frame of the *Titanic*. It did not come out of the iceberg. It was lying buried all the while only waiting the hour and the Voice that was to summon it to come forth.

Among the nations to-day this is the needed truth as it is the needed truth here in our own lives. There are boys here to-day who have been yielding to temptation, to whom God would give energies to withstand their enemy. In the nation there are even now capacities to conquer all the evils with which the nation abounds. Some day our children will look back and ask why we have allowed immorality to dominate the moral life of the land and why in the world we have endured the saloon so long. These things will be cleaned away some day and men will wonder then what their mothers and fathers were about

that they surrendered where that happier generation will not surrender but will achieve. The
needed capacities are buried of God in life, but
we are not willing to believe that they are there
or to have faith in Him to energize them.

Let me put the truth in yet a different way.

Last spring, just after Holy Week, I received
a very interesting letter from a friend who is one
of the best known and best loved judges in our
country. It was written on the Saturday between Good Friday and Easter Day, and he
said in it that he was pursuing the practice
which he had pursued for many years, of trying
in the interval between Good Friday and Easter
morning to eliminate Jesus Christ entirely from
his thought of life and of the world in order that
he might thus bring home to his own mind and
conscience more deeply the significance of Jesus,
and he said he could hardly wait for Easter
morning to come to escape from the oppressive
gloom and depression in which his spirit was as
a result of his enforced practice. And he begged
me, as one of his friends, to try this between the
next Good Friday and Easter Day and to see
what the experience would mean.

Oddly enough my own thoughts that same
day on which my friend was writing this letter
were exactly the opposite of his. He was thinking of Jesus Christ as extinguished, he was
thinking of all that He had come to be and to

do as gone, and he was trying to bring home to his own heart what this utter loss of Christ would mean. I was meditating, on the other hand, on that Saturday morning, on just the contrary idea. On Good Friday, the day before this Saturday, there had been a great Personality; now that Personality must be somewhere still. Personality does not die. The next day, on Easter morning, there was to be a great outburst of energy. That energy must be somewhere now. It will not be created to-morrow morning. It must be somewhere to-day waiting to come forth to-morrow. Where is it? And then I suddenly realized that it was all there, that all that was to break loose Easter morning was shut up inside that grave, that all the energies that were to peal across the world on the new day were there asleep in that tomb that Saturday. All the great love and power that had been had not been annihilated. It was there somewhere, only out of sight for a little while. And the great truth urged itself that all the dormant energies of life, all the enshrouded and enfolded powers are here now and always just as truly as they will be to-morrow when they awake, though for the hour they lie latent and unused.

Then I began to see, as one's thought ran easily on, that that Saturday between Good Friday and Easter Day was in reality a sort of symbol of the whole of history. For history, as

we look back upon it, is full of these repressions
and these emergences, and then perhaps repressions again, of great impulses and outbursts of
energy and of power. Now and then they are
for good, as when the Reformation broke across
men's minds, shattering their shackles, opening
old prison doors, allowing the enslaved human
spirit to come out and breathe the air of freedom. But why had it not come before? All
the great energies of God that burst forth in it
must have been here even before that hour.
And why did they have to subside afterwards?
They all *were* still? Why might they not have
gone beating their way onward and not have
ceased so soon?

Then also great explosions of evil come. We
look out across the world to-day and see all these
dogs of war unleashed. But these dogs of war
were not born the year before last. They had
been here all the time, only they were chained
and held in leash. Why were they not kept
chained and in leash? Why were they allowed
to break loose and go wild across the world in
their havoc and devastation? We know perfectly well that after a few months they are going to be chained again, and the great reconstructive processes will begin to make the world
anew. But why do these reconstructive forces
have to wait? They will not exist any more
truly then than they do to-day. Why not re-

lease them to-day to go out and do their creative
work in the world now? Why not on Saturday
let loose that which is to burst with creative freedom on the world on Easter morning?

And I saw that this was a symbol not of history only but also of human life, that every human life is just the mystery of the infolding of
latent capacities that are there wrapped up, the
infolding of great ends of which no man can
foretell. That is why, I suppose, a man feels
such awe every time he holds a very little child
in his arms. He does not know what it is that
he has in his arms, what it is that will some day
come bursting forth from that little child. That
must have been Mary's thrill in those early days
when she held her little one, knowing dimly and
far away, if not clearly, that she held in her arms
the mighty Redeemer of men. "When I see a
child," said Pasteur, "he inspires me with two
feelings: tenderness for what he is now, respect
for what he may become hereafter." Of personal life it is as true as of history. Vast latent
possibilities for good may come breaking forth.
Now and then they do, in some truth-loving,
unfearing, plain-speaking, God-obeying Martin
Luther. Or they may issue in some tranquil,
patient, loving-hearted, steady-spirited, immov-
able Lincoln. Goodness comes leaping forth,
and oftentimes we are tempted to think the surroundings, the circumstances, produced it. They

produced none of it. They gave it its opportunity and its chance, but it was all somewhere all the time and it might not have come forth if something inside had not released the spring of our will to God's will and let those great energies of good come pulsing out to do their work.

And the same thing is true of the inwrought and enshrouded capacities for ill. Jesus Christ laid off His limitations as well as His activities that Saturday in the grave; and He left His limitations there when He came out. Out of such Saturday graves in man's character it may be only the limitations that emerge. Out of many a man's life it is the dog that ought to be chained that is allowed to roam free, while all the possibilities for good and sacrifice and ministry are still-born inside. And sometimes, thank God, men discover all this latent ill within and lay on it the restraining and throttling hand. As godly old John Newton said when one day he saw a criminal being led by, " There, but for the grace of God, goes John Newton." He knew that everything that had escaped in that brother of his lay latent in himself, and he thanked God that a hand had been laid on all those inner capacities for evil and wreckage and that that hand held them in check and let only the good and the true and the pure go free.

There is something infinitely hopeful and encouraging in the principle of that Saturday in

our Lord's last week for every man and woman
of us, as we think of life's work and what we are
trying to get done in the world.   So many times
a thing seems all vain.   The teacher tried to
breed in the boy whom he taught a hate of lies
and a love of the truth, and he wrought with
tears and blood at his task, and the boy went
out from him and it seemed to him to have been
futile, this that he had done for him.   We put
ourselves out in this or that effort of service in
the hope of achieving this or that great end.
Every little while it seems to us to have been all
fruitless.   But wait.   It is only Saturday.   Easter
morning is going to break and the seed that was
sown in the ground in darkness and obscurity
will come forth then.   The life that was let go
for a little while, all that we did not see and
therefore thought had run sheer to waste, we
shall discover then will come pulsating back.
" No effort is wasted," said Pasteur.

It is a great joy of life to believe this, that
what Isaiah said is true through all the ages, by
the very principle of the life of God, that no
word of His will come back to Him vain or be
void, that it will accomplish the thing He pleases
and prosper in the errand whereon He sent it.
I received a letter the other day from a friend,
the Rev. Adolphus Pieters, who is a missionary
in Japan.   He had for very many years been engaged in an interesting work.   He published

advertisements of Christianity in the Japanese papers, and then occasionally printed a brief attractive account of what Christianity was, with the hope of arousing the curiosity of Japanese readers. At the end he would add that if any one were interested he might correspond with him. As a result of this work he came into correspondence with hundreds of men. In this recent letter he writes: " The total number of people who applied to us for tracts last year was 959, making the total from February, 1914, when the work began, to December 31, 1915, 3,590. There have been seven baptisms since my previous letter, and the total number to date is forty-five. Number Forty-Five is a most instructive case of the Lord's blessing resting upon what was, humanly speaking, a complete failure. The young man in question is a bright young student in the Normal School at this place, who was baptized a week ago last Sunday, after coming to my house off and on for two years, and getting a good deal of instruction. I did not reckon him among the results of the newspaper work, but after he was baptized he told me that he originally got interested in the Gospel when he was attending the primary school in his home town. Among his teachers was one named Okabe Katsumi, who had seen our advertisements and secured some tracts, among which were copies of the Gospels.

He did not care for them himself, and had given them to this boy, who was deeply impressed. In the course of time the boy graduated from school and went to Oita to attend the Normal, and he did so with the resolution already formed to look up the man who advertised in the papers and learn from him more about the Christian religion.

"When I heard that, I looked up the card index, and found among the 'dead' cards one for Okabe Katsumi. It was number 444, and he had applied for tracts in the spring of 1912, but in August he wrote that he had found something in our tracts that he did not like, and so had made up his mind to have nothing more to do with Christianity. So his card was marked in red ink, 'Closed August 12, 1913,' and filed away among the 'dead' ones—a complete failure, so far as any one could see. But it wasn't a failure. God knew better. On the fifth of March, 1916, a young man made public confession of his faith and was baptized as a sequel to that application of Okabe Katsumi in 1912.

"Such things sometimes make me look with something like awe upon my card index. What is going on beneath the surface? How is God working in the hearts of the 'failures,' or, if not in their hearts, through them in the hearts of others? It is one more proof that 'the foundation of God standeth sure, having this seal, The Lord knoweth them that are his.'"

Looking back across the years it could be seen that bread sown upon the waters returned again. Absolutely no energy goes to waste in this world,—no moral energy, no spiritual energy, any more than physical energy. All that is released goes about its work. Let us thank God, that there that Saturday morning in the dark of the grave all that broke free the next day *was*, and was not dead beyond the resurrection of life.

And the assurance that a man simply cannot do anything in vain is not only a word of great courage to us in the work that we are trying to do in the world, it is a word of hope and courage to us also in our own personal life and struggle for character. All the energy we need to accomplish anything that ought to be accomplished in us is in our reach. "All power," said Christ, "is given to me in heaven and in earth. I stand within at the centre of your life. Draw on me. Go out in the faith of that and do whatever your work is in the world. I have the energy that you need." All the energy that we require for any task in life or out of life is there, by token and assurance of the closed grave and resurrection, in Christ, waiting to be drawn upon by any man who wants to make use of it.

And all this is not the exaltation of human will, the setting up of a man's own resolution and high purpose. It is precisely the opposite of that. It is saying to a man: "There do not lie in the boastful surface of your life the power and the resources that you need. Retire upon God. You must get behind into the unplumbed depths where Christ waits. You must go back of the Easter morning in the grave, the unopened womb of the grave, to find it there. All of it is there in the now Risen Christ Who that Saturday morning awaited resurrection." This is simply making faith a living, acting reality by which a man works; so that he arises in the morning and can say: " O God, I have in Thee in me all the energy and strength that I shall need this day. No temptation can come to me to-day that I have not got the power in Thee, that I never have used yet, to draw upon, that will enable me to meet and conquer. No work will come to me to-day that is too much for me, no matter how exacting or unprecedented in my experience. There is power in Thee for me for this work that is come to me to do."

That Saturday morning, more vividly than any other day that brings back the triumph and pain and glory of Easter to us, makes a man assured that all the energies he needs are near by, that in God's own presence there are all the powers he wants, awaiting release by God's grace for all the necessities of his life. And if we could not believe this about the world we are living in to-day, surely a man could not go on living in it. If we had to surrender to the present order and temper of the world what would be left to uphold us? It is because we know it is Saturday night in human history that we can live through it.

We know that as in individuals so in all the races of mankind, God has planted these great dormant energies and powers. For scores and scores of years the Chinese had despaired of their power to throw off the opium curse. They knew it was sapping the very vitality of their land, and yet they wondered whether the day would ever come when they would have power enough to break those hateful chains that had been forged upon them, and get back their freedom. Twenty years ago, as we went to and fro in China, the most striking odour in the Chinese streets was the pungent stench of smoking opium. One could scarcely go into a Chinese city or walk in a Chinese highway without seeing the wretched shipwrecks who were the products of that vice. Poppy fields bloomed red over the Empire, and the race had almost come to despair. And what do we find to-day? There is scarcely a great poppy field in the Republic, scarcely a fume of opium that you can smell on the public street in any Chinese city. The bonfires flared across the land as they burned up the signs of the old bondage. A great race arose in power and in a massive moral upheaval shook itself free. God had planted the energies there that needed only the touch of a living faith in Him, a new assurance of the freedom of man to do His will, and in this matter the whole nation came out of its bondage into its liberty.

For generations men wondered whether slaves could ever be set free. We almost feared in our land here that slavery was a permanent institution. But there came a time at last when from the wrist of every American slave the chains fell away. It might have been generations before; it might not have been until generations after; only in that time appointed the moral energies awoke and came forth, and Saturday burst into Easter Day for the negro bondmen of America.

Precisely the same principle holds with regard to the things that we fight to-day. It holds with regard to the war on war. Some day we shall slay it. The kingdom of heaven, said Jesus, is among you. Well, let it loose. The kingdom of heaven will have no war in it; the kingdom of heaven will have no brothers cutting one another's throats in it; the kingdom of heaven will have in it no vice and lust dragging its slimy trail across men's hearths and hearts. If the kingdom of heaven is within, why not set it free, that we may live in it as well as have it buried inside of us! The world that we are living in is calling us to go back to that principle of Saturday morning and to believe that all we need to do the will of God is made available for us by God's grace now, if we will but obey.

And if some men say that all this is only to put in other words the theory of development, of historic evolution, why, what of it? Of course it is, but what is development except the drawing out of what has been folded in? What is evolution except the letting loose of what the mind of God Himself at the beginning had planted within,—when in the Lamb slain from the foundation of the world He poured the blood of Christ into humanity in order that humanity might be reinforced with the adequate energies to enable it to accomplish the thing that was God's first dream for it? Of course it is, and that is precisely the ground of Christ's constant appeal. "Come unto me," He said to men, believing that they could. "Unless you hear My call and follow Me, you cannot be My disciple." What meaning was there to His summons unless the power to respond was there in answer to His call? "I stand at the door of your inner being," said He, "and knock. I am there waiting."

And so to us to-day, just as clearly as in those days, His voice speaks: "Come out of your tomb, out of your chains, out of your narrowness, out of your limitations, out of your despairs, out of your dejections, out of your failures,—come out of them. The power of the endless life is here for you, if only by faith and love you will lay hold of it to-day." Is that not, after all, the great central message and the fundamental principle of Christ's Gospel to us, which He symbolized and illustrated in the shadow of the Saturday before the Easter victory? It is in one of the old hymns:

> " Low in the grave He lay —
> Jesus, my Saviour !
> Waiting the coming day —
> Jesus, my Lord !
> Death cannot keep his prey —
> Jesus, my Saviour !
> He tore the bars away —
> Jesus, my Lord !
> Up from the grave He arose,
> With a mighty triumph o'er His foes;
> He arose a victor from the dark domain,
> And He lives forever with His saints to
> reign :
> He arose ! He arose ! Hallelujah ! Christ
> arose ! "

And He arose once on Easter morning that on the Saturday before and on every day, every one of us might also rise out of the old, low, selfish, defeated life into the life through which are beating the victorious energies and the sufficient strength of God. Shall it be so with us?

> " Rigid I lie in a winding sheet,
>   Which mine own hands did weave,
> And my narrow cell is myself—myself,
>   Which yet I may not cleave.

> " And yet in the dawn of the early morn,
>   A clear voice seems to say,
> ' I am the Lord of the final word,
>   And ye may not say Me nay.

" ' Unloose your hands that your brother's need
        May ever find them free.
    Unbind your feet from their winding sheet;
        Henceforth they walk with Me.'

" And lo ! I hear ! I am blind no more !
        I am no longer dumb !
    Out from the doom of a self-wrought tomb,
        Pulsate with life, I come."

Yes, I may come if I will, by His life Who will
live again in me.

But the trouble is men do not believe this.
They do not believe in any latent capacities
adequate to the great task of life. They accept
the principle of surrender and incompetence.
They have nothing for God and God can make
no use of them. And I imagine that it is such
unbelief, such misgiving as to whether after all
we have any possibilities for God in us, the
undervaluation of God's need of us and power to
make and use us, that lead many of us to live
the futile, unfruitful, negative lives which we do
live. Men do not think their lives worth very
much. They do not deny that there are great men
and that great work is to be done in the world, but
they think that God requires only those, that He
builds His kingdom on a few outstanding figures,
that the common men can look after themselves,
and that they are not indispensable to God. If we
are to prevent this waste, and if we are to secure
the life without which God is impotent to build

His kingdom in the world, we must somehow bring home to men the recognition of the great truth that God cannot get along without every man and all of that man, and that every human life and all its buried powers are essential to God.

One of the great purposes of our Lord's coming here to earth was that He might show men the value of a man's life in the plan and thought of God. Even the most sacred and time-honoured institution our Lord weighed over against one man and found him outweighing the institution. What was His own example but the illustration of the immeasurable value of man? He did not come to teach the uselessness of human life, but its pricelessness. He did this by becoming a man Himself. And this principle of God's need of men and their latent possibilities is not mere theological theory. It is the hard historic fact that God has ever needed men and waited for them and for what they were the men to do for Him. Look at the great inventions, discoveries, achievements. What is the whole lesson of the Incarnation but that there are things that God Himself will not do except as He uses man? God Himself, we must say reverently, was communicable and a Saviour only as man. And His call to-day as it has been all through the years is for men who will believe that the thing God wants done can be done by Him through them. The Western Hemisphere was here before ever Columbus drew aside the veil and broadened the horizon of mankind. These great energies which drive the modern world were here from the beginning. We did not invent any of them. There is not an ounce of power in the world to-day that was not here when the world began. All that man has done has been simply to discover existing secrets. He has created no power. He has only found out what God has put here for him to find out. It took man a long time to discover this. But God waited for him. And God needs these finding men now as much as He has needed them at any time. He needs such men now to break open what is still concealed. The past has not exhausted all the heroisms, has not accomplished all the tasks. There are greater ones yet for the days that are, if God can only find His men.

Think how greatly God needs men to-day just to bring need and supply together in the world. You remember the incident in the life of our Lord as He came by the Pool of Bethesda where the sick lay, and spoke to one poor man lying on his pallet.

" Are you going in ? " said He.

" No," said the man. " I have no friend who will help me in and others get the benefit before I can come near."

There was the good, waiting to be gained, and here was the man, but he had no man to stand for him between the need and the supply. A few years ago a great famine raged just back from the coast of China. There were millions of Chinese families who were in want and hundreds of thousands died of starvation because there was not bread enough to feed them. Little children lay crying at the breasts of dead mothers by the roadsides. At that very hour the wheat was piled up at railroad stations in Argentina as high as church spires. There was grain enough to feed the starving millions in China. Here was the supply and there was the need, but where were the men? God had not men enough on whom to float the supply across to meet the need. What is true of outward need is true of inward need as well. There is never a want where there is not an adequate supply. No little child on this earth need go hungry because God has not put enough in this world to feed it. No human heart need go starved because there is not enough love to meet its wants. There is all the food and all the love that humanity needs. But there are lacking the men who for God will bring the supply to the demand. The human need in the world can be met by the supply only through men who will fill up the gap. God can do it only as men lend themselves to Him. That is why, through all the years, the call of God has been for volunteers. For every unique, external, individual call that has been given to men, you can find a million calls that have been just the answer of men to the great call of God for volunteers. And God surely values the volunteer above the conscript. Isaiah did not wait for any special coercive call. " Also I heard the voice of the Lord, saying, Whom shall I send, and who will go for us? Then said I, Here am I ; send me." That call was enough to cover him, and he answered it. There is so much work to be done that God cannot go marching through the world looking for individuals, performing new miracles by which each individual is to be thaumaturgically led up to his particular work. God's general way has been to picture before the eyes of His sons the work to be done and to wait for their hearts to leap in response, as Isaiah's leaped : " Lord, let me have a share in this work ' Here am I ; send me.' "

Men are indispensable to God to put meaning into the words in which He tries to tell His message to men. Words have no meaning of their own. Words mean only as much as one man puts into them, or another man takes out of them. The meaning of the word does not come from the word ; it comes from some life in which the word gets incarnated, or from some other life which interprets the word. What would the word " friend" signify to a man who had never had one? What does " tenderness " mean to one who has never seen a mother and her child? Or

what is "patriotism" to one who has never seen
or felt the contagion? You remember what the
eunuch said when Philip met him in the chariot
reading the prophet Esaias. "Understandest
thou what thou readest?" Philip asked. And he
replied, "How can I, except some man should
guide me?" Things mean nothing to men until
they are shown to them. Men go to China or
Japan and preach the Gospel. How is it done?
Why, they take words that have old meanings and
fill them with new and different meanings by living new ideas in deeds before the people. In our
colleges this year what meaning will honour,
truth and friendship have, except as these words
derive their meaning from the object lessons
in some men's lives? There are places where
honour means dishonour; where purity means
impurity; where truth means falsehood. These
noble words are confused with their very oppo-
sites because no man has incarnated their right
meaning in his life. That was one reason why
the incarnation was necessary nineteen hundred
years ago. There was no adequate religious or
spiritual vocabulary and never could have been
otherwise. If God had not come in the flesh,
men would not have had the ideas that we use
to describe God's coming in the flesh. To-day,
as then, God is dependent upon men in whom
He can put meaning into His message to the
world.

Men are indispensable in enabling God to get His other men. He gives men guidance for their lives But how? I appeal to your own hearts. How do we get the guidance of our lives? There are many who are sure of having divine guidance in their lives, surer of that than they are of any material thing, and yet, as we look back upon this supernatural guidance, we realize that it has all been mediated through men. We can name man after man who did for our lives, in smaller measure, just what that man of Macedonia did for Paul. We get our guidance through men. Saint Paul got his through a man. Through what man was it? Sir William Ramsay has no doubt whatever that the man whom Saint Paul saw in his dreams was none other than his friend Luke. A real man and a friend, and no ghost figure, was the man of Macedonia through whom God gave Paul his great missionary call.

It would be easy to recall the lives of great missionaries and point out how they received their divine guidance through other men—not even through a dream, far less through some miraculous vision, but through a brother man who came to talk with them, reasoned with them, and showed them the best way in which a man could use his life. Men are indispensable to God in order to guide other men into the work which God has for them to do. And one reason why there is such an awful waste of life to-day, why so many men, going out of the colleges, miss the highest work of their lives, is simply because there are not enough other men who recognize that they are indispensable to God in order that, through them, God may guide men to their highest and most efficient places.

Men are indispensable to God in bringing men to Jesus Christ. As men were brought to Christ by other men in the beginning, so has it been during all the succeeding years. The angels are willing to do what they can, but none of us have had any visible object lessons of what they do. Men have been brought to Christ always by other men. Imperfect lives are to be brought up to the Perfect Life, and to do this service Christ uses common men, just such as we are. That is what Paul conceived as the glory of his life, that he had the privilege of being the bond—no other beings in the universe being able to take that place—between men who had not found Christ and Christ hunting for His own.

Then God requires men now as He never required them in all the days gone by to bear testimony to the Deity of Jesus Christ. We know how little value our Lord attached to any accrediting evidences that did not come right out of pure, human personality. He discredited the advantages of bringing back Abraham from the dead, for example, to bear testimony to the truth. If men were not willing to accept adequate moral evidence, valid human testimony, they would not believe by miracle, He said. That is why He was so pleased with the confession of Simon Peter. "Blessed art thou, Simon Bar-jona; for flesh and blood hath not revealed it unto thee, but my Father which is in heaven." It rejoiced Him to get such testimony from a man who, in turn, had drawn it out of his own experience of God. There is no greater need in the world to-day than for a great body of men who know Christ to be God more surely than they know themselves to be men, and are able to go out and testify to what Christ can do with a definiteness and certainty greater than that of any other testimony they can bear, who can say what John said, "That which we have seen and heard declare we unto you." If there ever was a day when God was calling men to a great undertaking, He is calling them now to be His witnesses, unimpeachable, unflinching, to the unique personality, to the supreme divine character and power of our God and Saviour Jesus Christ.

And it is not only for great men that God is calling to do these indispensable tasks for Him. He wants the great men, no doubt, but He wants, more than that, the great mass of the common men. After all, the great man is only one man, and every little man counts just as many as one great man. Since God has to have all, one little man is as indispensable to the all as one great man can be. And until He has all, He cannot do what He purposes to do. It is only when we *all* come " unto the measure of the stature of the fullness of Christ" that any one of us can come. It is only when we " comprehend with *all* saints, what is the breadth, and length, and depth, and height " of the love of Christ, that any one of us can comprehend it. It is only when we *all* reflect as in a mirror the character of Christ that any one of us shall be " changed . . . from glory to glory, even as by the Spirit of the Lord." And the little men, as a matter of fact, are doing as much as the great. The night that Gough stood alone, with all hope gone, a drunkard in the gutter, an almost forgotten man laid his hand on his shoulder and said, " Man, there is a better life than this for you." The name of that man is remembered by a few, but forgotten by the multitudes who will never forget the name of John B. Gough, or cease to feel the glow of the fires which he kindled to blaze until the Judgment Day. Even a little man may fill such an indispensable place as that of helping God lay hold of a great man who will be one of the unmistakable forces of God.

And it is not only every man that is indispensable to God, but also every bit of every man. We cannot take some sections of our lives and eliminate them as though they were not indispensable to God. There can be no schism between a man's public and his private life. His hands and what he does with them, his imaginings and where they go when he is alone by himself without any coercing, these are just as much indispensable to God as a man's public worship or any of his activities in the open ministry of Christ's kingdom. It is every bit of the man—body, soul, and spirit—that is indispensable to God.

And if we are indispensable to God, we may be very sure that we are indispensable to the world also. If God needs us, the world needs us even more. It is waiting for the rising up of men who know that God needs them, and who hand themselves over completely to His uses. "The mightiest of civilizing agencies are persons," said Dr. Fairbairn, "and the mightiest civilizing persons are Christian men." Those men are doing most for the world who are doing most to make men aware of how necessary they are to God, and who are going up and down the lands allying men's lives to the eternal life and power of God. This is the greatest of all works—getting God His men. I heard Dr. J. Campbell Gibson tell the Chamber of Commerce in Glasgow of a visit which he made to a temple which had been turned into a modern school in inland China. Over the gate of the school were these words in Chinese : " If you are planting for ten years, plant trees ; if you are planting for a hundred years, plant men." Men are God's great interest and want.

What an opportunity this opens for every man of us ! We have thought of our lives as little, insignificant, trivial, of no consequence. There is One walking in the midst of us Who was speaking to Ezekiel. " I am hunting for a man," He is saying, " I am hunting for a man," and it is open to every one of us to rise up and say, " Lord, I am that man you are hunting for. Seek no further. Here am I. Have me for your man." Is that the answer that He is getting from us ?

LECTURE III

AN UNFRIGHTENED HOPE

IF we were asked what we considered to be the supremest motive in life, the motive which does actually exercise the largest control over human conduct, what would our answer be? A generation ago men would have answered glibly enough: "The desire for happiness." That was then supposed to be the one commanding motive of mankind. But it was not long before the answer seemed unsatisfactory and indefinite, because what brings happiness to one man brings misery to another, or what a man thinks will delight him in the end disappoints and such experiences issue in confusion. It was ethically indiscriminate also. The same motive covered moral contradictions, and men wanted some more consistent answer to the question. Nowadays those who look despondently at life often say in reply: "Avarice, —the desire for wealth." Or, those who look a little more deeply say it is not money, but the power that money represents that men desire, and that their real motive is to acquire sources of influence and control. Some who look at life more hopefully are likely to reply: "Love or friendship." That is the thesis of one of the noblest books of our generation, written by the late Dr. Henry Clay Trumbull, entitled "Friendship, the Master Passion." Doctor Trumbull told me once that when he first began the work on this theme he spoke about it to his friend Charles Dudley Warner, who said : " Trumbull, you cannot prove that thesis." After the book was done, Doctor Trumbull took the book to him and asked if he would read it. He read it, gave it back, saying: " Well, Trumbull, you have shown that it is true, after all." And that is a lovely view to take of life : that the motive that lies deeper than any other, and that really in the actual conduct of men and women is the most controlling, is the motive of unselfish friendship, of love.

But what would you say if instead of any one of these three or other answers that may suggest themselves, some one were to reply : " Not a bit of it. The motive that really controls human life, that does actually and not theoretically play the largest part in determining the conduct of men and women, is—*fear*." And before we pass that contention by it may be worth our while to look at it and ask whether, or how far, it is true.

Take it in the matter of dress, for example. Does not fear play a large part there,—either the fear of being unlike everybody else, or the fear of being too much like everybody else ? In every land, more even in civilized lands than in uncivilized, the element of fear enters into the small external characteristics of our daily living.

And in the matter of opinion. We speak of public opinion as though it were a free and stable and trustworthy thing. But the public opinion of one generation contradicts the public opinion of another generation. The public opinion of one section of the land denies the public opinion of another section, in the same way in which two sections of society in one community think in opposite ways. Why? Not because all the individuals of these particular generations, or sections, or portions of the community really and independently have thought the thing out for themselves, but because, held under the atmospheric constraint of fear, they are unwilling to break away from what is determined for them by the opinions in the midst of which they live. There is a good deal of pacifist opinion and a great deal more of militarist which is not free and personal at all, but simply herd intimidation. And a great deal of race prejudice and international suspicion is nothing but the miasma arising from cowardice or that bullying selfishness which is essentially cowardly.

And a great deal of religion is of the same character. The predominant element in many of the non-Christian religions is fear. It is so in all of the earlier or animistic religions, where men live in constant terror of the spirits that haunt the air or the world, and where a large element of their worship is shaped by that dominant principle of their religion, the dread of the unseen and the unexperienced. Even among us is there not a great deal, both of religious orthodoxy and of religious heresy, that is only the child of fear? There is a coercion of sound doctrine and there is a coercion of false doctrine, and a great many men and women belong to their school of religious opinion simply because they are afraid to break away from the companionship in which they have always been or to disagree with the associations which condition them.

Much religious conduct, too, springs only from the fear of one's environment. One of the saddest things which one meets in going out across the world is the great multitude, especially of young men, who, when they have left Christian lands and the environment and support of Christian surroundings, have simply collapsed in all their religious conviction and character. Asia is strewn from one end of it to the other with the wrecks of men who, while they were at home, supposedly were men of religious character and conviction, but who showed when they went away from home that it was not a matter of their own real selves at all. It was just a matter of their timid servility and acceptance of the conditions imposed upon them from without, so that once they were away from home and free to do as they pleased and had no longer the help and uplift of their surroundings, their environmental religion collapsed and they went in an entirely different way.

And I think if only we would go deep enough in our own lives, and be honest enough with ourselves to gain a clear insight into our motives and impulses, we would discover how large a part fear has played in us,—fear, of course, in all the wide range of its aspects, that shades off on the one side into arrant cowardice and on the other side into a mere hesitancy of character and timidity, but fear nevertheless. Some of us are even now cloaking the things that lie deepest in our hearts, because we are afraid to give expression to them. We go into communities, into circles, into conditions where what has been natural and real to us is unnatural and abnormal, and we hide our colours and conceal our principles. And we do things we ought not to do or we do not do the thing we know we ought to do simply because of fear.

I had an experience a little while ago when this diagnosis was confirmed to me. In a visit to one of our colleges, among the boys who came around to talk quietly was one whom I knew as one of the leading men in the life of the institution. He played on the eleven; he was president of his class. He was very timid about talking lest somebody should overhear, but when assured that we had the whole house to ourselves he took a letter out of his pocket and handed it to me.

He said: "Mr. Speer, I wish you would read this."

I looked at it and saw that it was written in a girl's handwriting, and said: "No, tell me about it."

"No," he said, "please read it. It will tell you a great deal better than I can."

So I opened his letter and began to read, substantially as follows:

"DEAR ———— :

"I know all about your life at ———— College, and I want to tell you what I think about you. You and I have known one another all our lives, and we have been good friends; but I think you are a coward and I think that I ought to tell you so."

I closed his letter and handed it back to him. His lips were quivering and his eyes were moist as he said:

"You can believe that when I got that letter it cut me all up, and the worst of it is that what she says is true."

His father was a minister; his mother was of the salt of the earth. He had grown up under the best influences of a clean and wholesome

Christian home, and he had slipped those strings. He had thought that it was manly to surrender to the current ideals of the college; that in cutting loose from the influence of his home he was doing a brave and courageous thing.   But the girl knew he was doing it because he was a coward and she had the courage to tell him so.   And he had come to see it in that light for himself.   In his college fraternity and in his own class, men were praising him because he had broken from the old enslavements of home and was living his own life like a man.   But he knew that he was nothing but a coward, who

> " Held that hope was all a lie
>   And faith a form of bigotry
>   And love a snare that caught him.
>   Then thought to comfort human tears
>   With sundry ill-considered sneers
>   At things his mother taught him."

And he had thought he was doing it because he was courageous, whereas the real motive was that of fear.   He was a coward, without courage enough to fly his own flag unflinchingly, to be and do the thing which in his heart, in the very fibres of his being, flesh of his mother's flesh, he knew was the thing he should be and do.

And if we would really look into our lives we should discover that fear plays a far larger part with us than we ever dreamed.   Men and women lie.   Why?   Simply because they are afraid of telling the truth and taking the consequences. Nine out of every ten falsehoods—perhaps ninety-nine out of every hundred—are the spawn of fear. And the same thing is true of sin, and of no small measure of unbelief, as well as of no small measure of pretended belief.

Our great need is the discovering of something that will cast fear out of our lives, that will enable us to walk unafraid in the open sunlight of His pathway Who bade men to be afraid of nothing. Think how greatly we need this emancipation from fear in the simple matter of loyalty to principle. There is so much of expediency and compromise and adaptation among us, so great reluctance to ruffle the smooth conventionalities of life, whereas what the world needs is men and women who can see right principle as principle, unconfused and undistorted, and then who, unafraid, will abide in that right principle.

How greatly, too, this is needed in the plain, commonplace matter of duty-doing! All around us much simple work waits to be done by men and women who, first of all, can see it, and then have the courage to do it. The obscure tasks that, after all, are the really great and worthy ones, how few there are to do them! There is a fine passage in Morley's essay on Rousseau in which he describes what real history is, and how much we make of history that really is not history at all, but simply the spectacular doings of

men who for the time being were deemed great
and who usually were engaged in war, whereas
the great bulk of life was not the life of warfare
at all. It was the life of peace,—of the quiet
agricultural people, of the tradespeople, of the
homes, which is not written up in any history at
all,—that was the real history of the world. The
men and the women who were doing earth's work
were not those who went out to battle or on great
expeditions, but those who, day by day, heroic-
ally, unflinchingly, and without fear of oblivion,
did the real business of the world. There are
some familiar lines of Lowell's in "Under the
Old Elm" that put the principle for us:

> " The longer on this earth we live
> And weigh the various qualities of men,
> Seeing how most are fugitive,
> Or fitful gifts, at best, of now and then,
> Wind-wavered, corpse-lights, daughters of the fen,
> The more we feel the high stern-featured beauty
> Of plain devotedness to duty, steadfast and still,
> Not fed with mortal praise,
> But finding amplest recompense
> For life's ungarlanded expense
> In work done squarely and unwasted days."

And take this matter of Christian service that
lies before the thought of every earnest young
life. Why are so many of us going to be, in the
cities and homes from which we came, the same
useless driftwood that we have been? Why?
Simply because of our want of courage to face

the work that needs to be done there, and to undertake that work without fear that we cannot do it, without fear that God will desert us in attempting to do it, without fear of the irregularity and uniqueness of our being seen engaged in it. Throughout the world Christ waits for men and women to-day, as He waited for them—and so often in vain—while He was here on earth. Who will hear His call now? "Lay aside your fear and trust Me to be with you and to enable you to do the thing. Come and take up My task after Me."

Some of us would dread to go out to live among the Chinese or Mohammedan peoples, so far away. But we would not dread going out to live in the legation, nor would we dread it much if we were to be employed in some great commercial enterprise. Yet the geography would be precisely the same, and our dangers and friendlessness would be far greater. But we would not fear all that, because others would think it natural and appropriate for us. But this other thing—the missionary call—would be so exceptional, so unusual, so fantastic, even fanatical, that we would fear to do any such dreadful thing! But which life of us is worth mentioning in the same breath with the life of God's Son Who came into a carpenter's home in a wretched little Jewish village amid an outcast race, in a bare remote corner of the earth, and lived there among peasant folk and farmers, pent up in the charnel house of humanity, and Who was willing to count His equality with God not a prize jealously to be retained, Who emptied Himself and took on Him the form of a servant and became obedient unto death, even the death of the Cross? The contrast between our life, with all its privileges, to-day and the most squalid African village is invisible over against the contrast between what Christ laid down and what Christ took up for the love He bore us and His world.

And we need greatly this fearlessness in our confession of Him,—that, without concealing Whom we follow and Whose servants we are, we should go out now, openly to avow our discipleship and the vow we have taken of loyalty to our Lord Jesus Christ! Think how many betrayals of Him there have been, and how much of putting afresh to shame the Son of God and crucifying Him anew by men and women who had said they were going to follow Him faithfully, just as Simon said he was resolved to do on that very night in which before the cock crew he denied his Lord. Shall we not go out into the coming days with something in us that casts out this fear?

We look with longing and admiration upon such deliverance from fear when we find it in other lives. I was in Edinburgh during the South African war, just after the battle of Maegersfontein, and was staying in the house of friends. There was one little boy in the family named after Prof. Henry Drummond. I had been in the library all the afternoon, the very room in which Sir James Simpson discovered chloroform, and then had gone into the drawing-room for afternoon tea. The boy and his governess were the only other members of the household who came down. He and I fell to talking about the war. I asked him: "What do you think about the war in South Africa?"

"Well," he said, "I did not think much about it at the beginning; I did not think about it much until a friend of mine was killed."

"Yes," I said, "who was the friend?"

"General Wauchope."

He was, as you know, the commander of the Black Watch, and the Black Watch had been recruited from Edinburgh. The boy told me about the regiment and its fate, and shortly after his story was filled up by an Oxford man who had been in Edinburgh when the tidings of the battle came. He said every shop was closed, and along the streets little knots of men were gathered, and you could see the sobbing of strong men everywhere. There was scarcely a great family in Edinburgh that had not been touched. And yet, at the same time, all through the city there was a subdued sense of moral elevation, as though something had lifted the character and temper of the city. They sorrowed in what had gone out from them; but they rejoiced in the way that it had gone. That regiment had been organized as a Scotch kirk. The chaplain was the minister of the kirk. The officers constituted the kirk's session. I believe almost every man in the regiment was a member of the kirk, and I was told that as they went down through the streets of Cork to embark for South Africa, although not under orders or restraint, the men walked with arms on one another's shoulders, singing:

> " I'm not ashamed to own my Lord,
> Or to defend His cause,
> Maintain the honour of His Word,
> The glory of His laws."

And when they were disembarked at Cape Town and were taking their train to go to the front, they went on board singing the old Gospel soldier's hymn:

> " When the roll is called up yonder,
> I'll be there."

They were sent right up and almost at once into that fateful battle. General Wauchope knew somebody had blundered, and he said to the men: " Men, do not blame me for this." And without any fear they went into the ending from which no soldier such as they would draw back, unafraid of anything that might come to them because unashamed to own their Lord and unfearing to follow Him.

Of such as those are we to be? Or will temptation intimidate us, and the tone of the conversation of the men and women with whom we mingle pull us down and cause us to fold our colours up and lay them away, as the man did whom the sneer of a serving maid caused to deny the Lord Who was dying for him?

Where are we to find that which will drive out this fear? "Perfect love casteth out fear. . . . He that feareth is not made perfect in love." From how many of our hearts to-day will the perfect love of Him Whom we call Master and Lord expel all fear? Let it be so now. Not years afterwards, when other things shall have palled upon us, years that shall have brought their dulling influence with them, but now, in all the full strength and richness and glory and eagerness of our lives, let us admit the perfect love that shall cast out fear and send us out the kind of men and women Christ would have us be, to join the great company of men and women and girls and boys who, unfearing,

> " . . . . climbed the steep ascent of Heaven,
> Through peril, toil and pain.
> O God, to us may grace be given
> To follow in their train!"

Christian character needs this conquest of fear and it needs the love which is one of the deep springs of such conquest. It needs also in our day an immensely more practical use of the principle of hope, a principle almost totally neglected in theology and made nothing of in our codes of conduct or in our creeds. Paul had a far deeper insight into the human heart and a vastly richer grasp on life. " Now abideth faith, hope, love, these three," said he.

Paul rendered a large service when he condensed the central ideals and principles of Christianity in this way. The human mind is very fond of formulas. If it had not been for some authoritative, simplifying word like this, we might have gone on to construct all sorts of prescriptions like the threes and sixes and tens and fifteens with which we are so familiar in Buddhism. And yet the service which Paul rendered is not without its dangers, for men are prone to simplify further and to see whether the three cannot be reduced to one, or to arrange the order and proportions of the three, or to contend alone for that which some one of them signifies at the expense of the other two. Paul's own words should have saved us from such folly, for he said quite clearly that one of these three was the greatest, " And now abideth faith, hope, love, these three ; and the greatest of these is love." And yet his own doctrine elsewhere has been used to correct and to counteract his expressed judgment here, and through the years we have had our theologies constructed in disregard of the domination of that one of these three principles which Saint Paul exalts. It has been in terms of faith, and faith given a very definitive construction, that our theological thinking with regard to Christianity has been chiefly done. Little by little however the proportions have changed, and now love, as one of the three great fundamental principles of Christianity, is coming to its own, not as a principle of action only but as a regulative principle also of our thought.

But it is a strange thing that no one has ever arisen, apparently, to say of hope what the intellect of the Church, over against Paul's judgment, has been prepared to say of faith. He declared that of these three, love is the greatest. The current opinion of Christian thought through the Christian centuries has contended that faith was the greatest. What would men say if some one should arise now to restore the proportions, who would make bold to declare, " Now abideth faith, hope, and love; and the greatest of these is hope"? Surely the day will come some time when hope will come to its own, when the Christian heart and mind will no longer be content to construe its interpretation of Christianity in terms either of love or of faith, or of love and faith together, but will insist that these three abide—faith and love and hope.

And when a man stops for a moment to think, to disengage himself from the unscrutinized conventions, he begins to realize immediately that he has no faith and love unless he makes larger room for hope in his thinking and feeling than has been allowed to us.   For there cannot be any faith detached from hope.   You can conceive of faith in three different ways.   You may think of it in its primary form, in its primary form in the New Testament at least, as personal trust, as the confidence that exists between two personal spirits.   But even so, can you think of it without hope?   If I have no hope of seeing Him in Whom I trust, of consulting with Him, or serving Him, of entering into a deeper and enlarged fellowship with Him, will not my personal trust soon empty itself of reality?   Or, secondly, you may think of faith as the writer of the Epistle to the Hebrews does, as the "substance of things hoped for"; in which without any flinching, he binds faith up with hope in terms that cannot be severed.   And, thirdly, if you go on to the rest of his definition, "the substance of things hoped for, the evidence of things not seen," still faith is undetachable from hope; for, as Paul says in another passage, "We are saved by hope: but hope that is seen is not hope: for what a man seeth, why doth he yet hope for?   But if we hope for that we see not, then do we with patience wait for it."   And you cannot detach love from hope or have anything that is real in the experience of love unless it inevitably leads a man on into those things that clearly were in Paul's mind when he spoke not of faith and love only but also of hope.   I ask any man's heart if it is possible to divorce hope from love.   I suppose in one sense it may be, and that you can speak of a hopeless love.   Henry Martyn's heroic and tragic life was the unfolding of a hopeless love. But how different that is from love that is undershot with hope.   One looks towards evening to see the children waiting as he comes home.   The workman lives in the hope of all that is there of joy and confidence and perfect trust inside his home.   Love would be a sorry thing to-day if it were stripped of the hopes that give it its sweetness and its joy.

And it is not only faith and love that root themselves inseparably in hope, and that lose their fragrance and meaning if they do not continue to draw both out of hope, but regarding almost everything else that is dearest and most precious to us in life, does it not spring from this same great treasury?   In one of the chapters of the Epistle to the Romans we find Paul again and again, in his efforts to bring his message out to those to whom he writes, describing God in different terms of speech.   He begins by speaking of Him as the God of comfort, the God of patience, and then he goes on to speak of Him as the God of hope. "Now the God of hope fill you with all joy and peace in believing, that ye may abound in hope." And then he closes by speaking of the God of peace who is to order all hearts. Quite evidently in his thought these things all run together, as again he writes: " Be ye sober. Walk as children of light. Put on the breastplate of faith and love, and for an helmet the hope of salvation." Joy and gladness and confidence and trust and hope,—all are rooted each in the other in his own mind and experience. The best that we have got in life springs from the fountains of hope.

We do not wonder, accordingly, that the old religious experience and the richer Christian experience, when it came, conceived and spoke of God as the God of love and the God of hope. They never spoke of Him as the God of faith. The old Hebrew idea of Him was as the ground-rock of their hope. "O hope of Israel," was their cry. The lovely thing is that that burst from the lips of the man who mourned for his nation : " O the hope of Israel, the saviour thereof in time of trouble." " Hope thou in God : for I shall yet praise him, who is the health of my countenance, and my God." God Himself when He comes to let Himself be richly known to men makes on them the impression of a great and joyous and glad and eager and boundless hope.

And when we turn away from such clews as

these and look right into the face of life to ask
what the powers and services and functionings
of hope in the actual life of man and in the life
of the world are, we realize that all this exultant
hope has its deep grounding in the actual living
needs of men. It is by hope—the New Testament is unequivocal about it, and our own experience answers to that word—it is by hope that
we are saved. Not in one passage in the New
Testament can you find the declaration that we
are saved by faith. We are saved "by grace
through faith," but Paul is flat-footed in his declaration that we are saved by hope. And the
moment a man looks life square in the face he
sees why it should be so. Were it not for hope
there could not be any saving that were worth a
man's while. There might be a clearing up of
the past; we might secure something like a clean
conscience; but there could not be any confidence, any ease, any rest, as over against the
tragic problem of life, if a man could not look
out into the future—which is really the thing he
now has to deal with—with boundless hope.
Salvation is just that thing. It is not cleaning
up our lives from the point of view of the past,
just for the sake of cleaning up our lives; but it
is the hope that for the sake of our future God
is going to live in us a saving life.

All this is true whether we think of salvation
as it comes penetrating our lives and dealing

with such problems as in shame and self-distrust we think of in our hours of recollection and penitence, or whether we think of it as something reaching out into the expanding experience of the future.   Either way, salvation is a matter of hope.   There is a lovely touch in one of Paul's epistles where he says : " Having therefore these promises, dearly beloved, let us cleanse ourselves from all filthiness of the flesh and spirit, perfecting holiness in the fear of God."   What do you think of that motive?   He does not say, "Seeing that our sin is so black and abhorrent as it is, seeing that the past is so shameful and unworthy as it is, let us cleanse ourselves."   " My brothers," he said, " seeing we have such promises "—that is, " that the hope is so bright, that there is no ground for despair, that we can believe victory can actually be achieved by us, seeing that we have these hopes, let us cleanse ourselves in growing holiness."

And then when those first Christian men came to look not only at this present purging of life which should leave it rich and fragrant and glorious but out upon the wide ranges of the untried and the unforeseeable, they still construed salvation in terms of hope.   " Now are we the sons of God, and it doth not yet appear what we shall be : but we know that, when he shall appear, we shall be like him ; for we shall see him as he is.   And he that hath this hope in him purifieth himself, even as he is pure." It is so because there is in front of us the dear voice calling, the voice that says to every one of us: "Man, let that old past go now. It is done and gone beyond recall. Come out with Me. There is a new road for your feet and Mine, a new tale that is to be unfolded now, a new story, the contradiction of the old. Let the past go now, and come and walk with Me in the limitless hope of the new ways."

And it is not only by hope, as a simple downright matter of fact, that men are saved and held fast to the Saviour; it is by hope also that men are nerved and empowered. In the hour of darkness, it is what lights all the darkness and makes it possible for men to bear. "Yes," we say to ourselves in the hour of pain, "I know; but I can stand it, for after this comes something that is different from this." That is what the honest doctor says to us when he deals with us. "Now hold steady for a moment. I am going to cut and it will hurt dreadfully. But just wait. Beyond the pain lies freedom from pain." And we say, "Yes, doctor, cut. I can stand it." In a moment the anguish is over. We endure in that hope. Has it not always been so? For a little while the mother bears her anguish and her pain for the joy and hope that a child is born into the world. For a little while Jesus bore the loneliness and the anguish of His grief and the

shadow and the pain and the disgrace of His
Cross, because, looking over it, He saw the glory
that awaited Him and the world, and He endured all this, this anguish of the Cross, for the
joy that was set beyond. " Therefore," says
Paul, " we rejoice in tribulation, in being flailed,
in being pressed down as grapes in the wine-
press, in being put through discipline and strain,
we rejoice in all that, because we know that
tribulation worketh steadfastness, steadfastness
experience, and experience hope, and hope
maketh not ashamed."

And you know the paradox, and the glory of
it, is that the darker you make the shadows the
more triumphantly hope laughs in the midst of
them.   The more difficult you make the night,
the more hopeful and enticing is the sure confidence of the dawn that is not far away.   Our
word, " Cheer up !   The worst is yet to come,"
is as deep a Christian word as was ever yet
spoken.   Be glad, because darker things lie just
ahead and then light beyond.   Thank God that
you are counted worthy for tribulations like
these ; for these are what wash white a man's
robes and make him fit to walk after the Lamb
whithersoever He goes, in company with the
men whose lips have never known a lie.

All this is put finely for us in " The Ballad of
the White Horse," the best piece of work Ches-
terton has done.   They were as dark days as

ever had been in English history. Tide after
tide of invasion from Norse and Dane had come
pouring in. Again and again Alfred had called
his men and gone out and fought, and each
time in vain. Now, as he sits on his little island
in the Thames among the reeds, the news comes
to him that the Danes are on their way for a
fresh invasion of his land. He kneels in prayer
and asks the Virgin Mother whether he ought to
go out yet once more. Again and again, he
tells her, he has gone out in hope, and each time
in the confidence that victory would be his, and
each time he has come back defeated, his men
killed, and his people to sink lower after
each despair than the time before. And yet,
as he prays to her he says that if she will give
him one word of assurance, he will go again.
But only this, as she stands by his side, will she
say,

> " I tell you naught for your comfort,
>   Yea, naught for your desire,
> Save that the sky grows darker yet,
>   And the sea rises higher."

And there that day among the reeds under the
promise only that the night was going to be
blacker than he had ever known, that storms
fiercer than he had ever breasted were coming,
Alfred rises up to do what he had never done
under the old assurance of easy victory,

" Up over windy wastes and up
    Went Alfred over the shaws,
Shaken of the joy of giants,
    The joy without a cause."

And as his men saw him coming, they thought it was with the old vain word of a sure victory, and they were about to tell him in advance that if he came with such a message they would follow him no more. But not now was Alfred's word the easy word.   No, but—

" This is the word of Mary,
    The word of the world's desire ;
 No more of comfort shall you get
 Save that the sky grows darker yet,
    And the sea rises higher.' "

And in front of that darkening sky and that rising sea his men rose up to go with him, and this time, from the darkest night they had ever known, came the bright morning of their lasting victory. Thank God, we are not called out on any soft errand under the incitement of bright choices, but challenged by great difficulties, black nights and rising storms, to work in the hope of that which is invisible and which lies beyond. It is by hope, and hope that lies behind impenetrable clouds, that men are nerved and empowered. It is because the world is so black and dark to-day that we walk out into it smiling in its face, knowing that behind all this the morning the more surely waits, the morning in which the men believe who have faith and love and hope.

And it is by hope that our comforts are drawn down into our lives when the darkest of all days come, and everything is quiet about the house and the little feet that had run to and fro are still. We say, "Yes, a little while and then those angel faces will smile, that I have loved and lost and love." What would we do in those hours if it were not for the sure hope? Saint Paul lays his own heart open to all his friends in one of his epistles: "But I would not have you to be ignorant, brethren, concerning them which are asleep, that ye sorrow not, even as others which have no hope. For if we believe that Jesus died and rose again, even so them also which sleep in Jesus will God bring with him. For this we say unto you by the word of the Lord, that we which are alive and remain unto the coming of the Lord shall not prevent them which are asleep. For the Lord himself shall descend from heaven with a shout, with the voice of the archangel, and with the trump of God: and the dead in Christ shall rise first: then we which are alive and remain shall be caught up together with them in the clouds, to meet the Lord in the air: and so shall we ever be with the Lord. Wherefore comfort one another with these words."

And as for us who are in the full flush and

possession of all that we have, it is by hope that we draw our comfort for our struggle. As against the background of our defeats and failures, we say to our own hearts: "Well, wait, just wait; my time will come. No matter how much of this there has been, some day my hope will be fulfilled. It is sure that something else than this there will yet be." William Henry Green became the outstanding Hebrew scholar in America. He was plucked when he entered college in Latin and Greek. At Lafayette College for months and months he found himself beaten on the very battle-field where he stood at last the first man in the land. At Lexington, Virginia, several years ago, I went to the grave of General Lee in the chancel of the chapel of his college and then I went out to the grave of Stonewall Jackson on that little hill. One of his townsmen was telling me the story of Jackson and how by hope he wrested triumph out of his uttermost failure. He had been teaching in the military academy, and had just been about to give up his work because he had no gift of discipline. He could not maintain order in his own classroom, my friend said, and was about to surrender his career as a teacher, because he thought he was incapable there. Then the war broke out, and within twelve months Stonewall Jackson was the most famous disciplinarian on earth. On the very field where the man's failure had been most clear, there he achieved his richest and greatest victory, by hope. And so we comfort our hearts here to-day. "Yes," we say to memories of which we are reminded in our searching hours, "the evil and unworthy imaginings and desires cling to us still, but it will not be forever. Some day, no matter how often I have failed, if I live in hope, it will come to me, the clean thing that the Lord said should be mine."

And last of all, there is nothing adequate for us in the way of actually moulding men and doing that with life which we were set here to do unless we can go to the work in the spirit in which our Lord and Saint Paul entered it. If I have no hope for another man, I cannot awaken any hope in him for himself. Unless I believe in him, how can he believe? The glory of Christ was that, though He knew just what was in man, and saw all the weaknesses and the slavery and the impurity and the unwholesomeness, though He saw all this in man, He shut His eyes to it deliberately and believed in the better capacities and possibilities that were there and that He by His grace and His power could plant and nurture and bring out until all that old baseness that had been the man was not the man any more, and all this new purity that had not been the man was the man, and Simon was turned at last out of his putty into rock and stone.

I do not know whether the apostles were conscious or not of what was happening to them. Maybe they did not appreciate their Master, but one likes to think that they must have done so, and that often they would go off by themselves and one would say: "Andrew, is He not just great? Did you ever meet any one like that before? Did you see what He did this morning? He just shut His eyes completely to that meanness that He saw in me, and that I saw the moment I let it out, too, and He pretended that He never saw it at all, and He believed in me when He knew and I knew there was nothing there to believe in. Is He not wonderful? He will make a man of me yet." And to this day He is still doing just what He was doing then. In this place now He is doing just that thing. He is shutting His eyes to what we do not want Him to see and opening them to what only He can see in us. And His law must be our law.

I can put it in a little story that a friend of some of us, George Truett, told to a little group some years ago in a western city. "I am fond," he said, "of recalling the first soul it was ever given me to win to Jesus. I was a lad barely grown and a teacher in the mountains of Carolina. One morning, as we were ready for prayers in the chapel, there hobbled down the aisle to the front seat a boy of about sixteen years old. He was an eager, lonely-looking lad. I read the Scriptures and prayed and then sent the teachers to their classes. But my little cripple lad stayed. I supposed that he was a beggar. And I said to myself, 'Surely this boy deserves alms. His condition betokens his need.' So I went to him at recess and said, 'My lad, what do you want?' He looked me eagerly in the face and said: 'Mr. Truett, I want to go to school. Oh, sir, I want to be somebody in the world. I will always be a cripple. The doctors have told me that, but,' he said, 'I want to be somebody.'

"He had won me. He told me of their poverty, and that was taken care of. I watched that lad for weeks and weeks. How bright his mind was! How eager he was to know! One day I called him into my office and said to him: 'My boy, I want you to tell me something more about yourself.' He told me how, a few months before, his father had been killed in the great cotton mill where he worked, and the few dollars he had saved up were soon gone. They tried to do their best in the county where they were, but found it difficult; so his mother said one day: 'Let us move to the next county, where they do not know us. Perhaps we can do better where we are not known.' So they moved and now he had come into my school. He said, 'I want to help mother, and I want to be somebody in the world; so I made my appeal to you to come to your school.' It was time in a moment for the bell to ring for books. I laid my hand on the head of the little fellow and said to him: 'Jim, I am for you, my boy. I believe in you thoroughly, and I want you to know that I love you, my boy.' And when I said that last word, the little pinched face looked up into my face almost in a lightning flash, and he said: 'Mr. Truett, did you say you loved me? Did you say that?' I said, 'I said that, Jim.' And then with a great sob he said: 'I did not know anybody loved me but mother and the two little girls. Mr. Truett, if you love me, I am going to be a man yet, by the help of God.' And when a few Friday nights afterwards I was leading the boys in their chapel meeting, as was the custom, I heard the boy's crutches over in the corner. There Jim sat, in a chair away from the other boys to protect his leg. And a little later he got up, sobbing and laughing at the same time, and said, 'Mr. Truett, I have found the Saviour, and that time you told me you loved me started me towards Him.'" And then our friend added, "Brothers, working men in the shops and everywhere are dying for love. Your grammar may be broken, your plans may be imperfect, your machinery may be crude, your organization may be rough; but if you love men and pour your hearts out to them honestly and directly, there will be a response that will fill your hearts with joy and heaven with praises."

And the need and functions of hope should be

viewed in no narrow personal way. We want to-day men who have a large and courageous faith in God for the nation and the world. Of recent years a mood of pessimism has spread through America. In one sense it represents a wholesome reaction from the spirit of braggadocio and spreadeagleism of an earlier day. So far it is wholesome. We need to be sobered and made modest and quiet in our national spirit. But it is a bad thing when a nation loses the zest of a great consciousness and a brave patriotism, and thinks meanly of what God can do with it. Our nation needs now not a timid and fearful sense of its impotence and incapacity, but a realization that, whatever its difficulties and defects, God has a mission for us which only we can fulfill for Him. For this mission those men must be the nation's soul of hope and expectation who know that our greatest duty and service lie ahead of us and are waiting to be grasped by men whose hearts face the untried without fear.

And now shall we have this hope that nothing can slay? Do we want it? Well, it is so near to us that we do not need to reach out after it. You know where it is, "Christ in you, the hope of glory." "The Lord Jesus Christ," as Saint Paul says in the opening words of his first Epistle to Timothy, "The Lord Jesus Christ, our hope." This hope is not something that we work up out of the fragments of moral ideals

that we find lying around in our lives or our
nation. Jesus Christ is the hope for a man and
a people. If we want it, why not now take Him?
Genuinely, I mean, in a deep, living, religious
way, take Him in His fullness of life? God and
the nation want the men who are filled with His
courage and hope:

" God's trumpet wakes the slumbering world,
   Now each man to his post.
   The red cross banner is unfurl'd,
   Who joins the glorious host? Who joins the glorious
      host?
   He who in fealty to the truth
   And counting all the cost
   Doth consecrate his gen'rous youth,
   He joins the noble host! He joins the noble host!

" He who, no anger on his tongue
   Nor any idle boast,
   Bears steadfast witness 'gainst the wrong,
   He joins the sacred host! He joins the sacred host!
   He who with calm, undaunted will
   Ne'er counts the battle lost
   But though defeated battles still,
   He joins the faithful host! He joins the faithful
      host!

" He who is ready for the cross,
   The cause despised loves most,
   And shows not pain or shame or loss,
   He joins the martyr host! He joins the martyr
      host!
   God's trumpet wakes the slumbering world.
   Now each man to his post.
   The red cross banner is unfurled.
   We join the glorious host! We join the glorious
      host! "

LECTURE IV

THE JOY OF THE MINORITY

THERE are two forms of disloyalty. One is flinching, the other is compromise. Of course, the compromiser will never allow that he is disloyal. He is a practical man who realizes that theories and ideals have to be adapted to a practical world, and he gives up a part, and as unimportant a part as possible, in order that he may gain the rest. He feels himself quite capable of judging how much to give up and what part may rightly be given up. He will simply abate the unreason of a God who demands all righteousness, and to Whom the whole truth is truth. Let us set up against such men the uncompromising principle of the duty of non-compromise. It is a principle from which the wisest and best of men are sometimes won away in the supposed interest of the great ends which they seek, and for which they feel that they may rightly sacrifice subordinate issues. There is what some regard as a striking incident of this character in the life of that uncompromising man, Saint Paul. It is an exciting and instructive story. This is the way it is told in the twenty-first chapter of Acts (vs. 17–30):

"And when we were come to Jerusalem, the brethren received us gladly. And the day following Paul went in with us unto James; and all the elders were present. And when he had saluted them, he rehearsed one by one the things which God had wrought among the Gentiles through his ministry. And they, when they heard it, glorified God; and they said unto him, Thou seest, brother, how many thousands there are among the Jews of them that have believed; and they are all zealous for the law: and they have been informed concerning thee, that thou teachest all the Jews who are among the Gentiles to forsake Moses, telling them not to circumcise their children, neither to walk after the customs. What is it therefore? they will certainly hear that thou art come. Do therefore this that we say to thee: We have four men that have a vow on them; these take, and purify thyself with them, and be at charges for them, that they may shave their heads: and all shall know that there is no truth in the things whereof they have been informed concerning thee; but that thou thyself also walkest orderly, keeping the law. But as touching the Gentiles that have believed, we wrote, giving judgment that they should keep themselves from things sacrificed to idols, and from blood, and from what is strangled, and from fornication. Then Paul took the men, and the next day purifying himself with them went into the temple, declaring the fulfillment of the days of purification, until the offering was offered for every one of them.

"And when the seven days were almost completed, the Jews from Asia, when they saw him in the temple, stirred up all the multitude and laid hands on him, crying out,

Men of Israel, help : This is the man that teacheth all men everywhere against the people, and the law, and this place ; and moreover he brought Greeks also into the temple, and hath defiled this holy place. For they had before seen with him in the city Trophimus the Ephesian, whom they supposed that Paul had brought into the temple. And all the city was moved, and the people ran together ; and they laid hold on Paul, and dragged him out of the temple : and straightway the doors were shut."

And that was the disastrous end of this conscientious experiment. Paul never tried another like it. Perhaps there is a construction of the story which forbids the idea that it was compromise but it suffices at any rate to raise the whole question of the wisdom of compromise as a principle of action. It is the one incident in Paul's life where he might be thought even for a moment to have embarked on that course. Wherever else we see him, he is a man of firm and unflinching principles, who made no concealment of what he believed, and did not try to adjust his convictions and practices to other convictions and practices that were at variance with them.

In the second chapter of Galatians, you will remember, Paul is telling of a visit he made to Jerusalem some time before with Barnabas and Titus, in which they went up to consider these very questions. Some of the brethren in Jerusalem had endeavoured to persuade Paul to have Titus, who was a Gentile, circumcised, and Paul says, " To whom we gave place . . . no, not for an hour."   And then he tells of the time when Peter came to Antioch and he withstood him to his face because he had been a trimmer and compromiser ; for Peter, acting on the generous impulse of his own heart as to what was right, had indeed bravely eaten with the converted Gentiles, but when some men came down from Jerusalem who were close to James, he withdrew himself from the Gentiles, fearing, no doubt, that it might injure him in Jerusalem.

Paul does not say anything in any letter about this particular incident in Jerusalem, in which, for the one time in his life, he was overpersuaded by his friends and put in a position where he was very much misunderstood, and where he appeared to be compromising the great prin- ciples in which he earnestly believed.   We know what the far-reaching consequences were.   A great deal of trouble was brought into his life by this act.   It was out of it that all those succeed- ing events came which took him at last to Rome to be tried before Cæsar.   Some may say that these results were good.   Undoubtedly God led Paul's course on, but we may believe that God might have had even greater things for him to do if only he had in this incident pursued his customary course.

But we want to go far beyond the question as to whether the consequences may ever appear to justify acts of compromise. A course of action is right or wrong, not according to the consequences, but according to its conformity or unconformity to the character of God. And the point now raised is whether it is ever right for us to compromise our own firm convictions of truth and principle.

Now, the world tells us that such compromise is to-day absolutely unavoidable. Men and women, we are assured, cannot get along in a world like this without adaptations. If it is meant by this only that we are often obliged to adapt ourselves to that with which we do not agree, why, of course, we have to assent, because we are in a world of give and take of which we have to be a part, and it is necessary for us to live our life and do our work in this world. Here in many of our communities, for example, the saloons flourish. There is not one of us here in this audience who believes that it is wise that the saloon should exist under the protection of the government, but we have to live in a land where the principle with which we disagree prevails, and the only way we can escape is to go to some other land, and we would only find there some other principle with which we could not agree. We cannot live at all unless we are willing to adjust ourselves to an actual world. "Compromise" when used as the principle of such adjustment means simply that we must of necessity find room for ourselves among the crossing strands of life. "All government," says Burke, "indeed every human benefit and enjoyment, every vital and every prudent act, is founded on compromise and barter." "It cannot be too emphatically asserted," says Spencer, "that this policy of compromise alike in institution, in action and in belief which especially characterizes English life is a policy essential to a society going through the transition caused by continuous growth and development." And Emerson remarks, "Almost all people descend to meet. All association must be a compromise, and, what is worst, the very flower and aroma of the flower of each of the beautiful natures disappears as they approach each other."

If it is meant by compromise that we have to live under conditions with which we do not agree and to which we must adjust ourselves, why, of course, we must assent to that—it is perfectly obvious; but we do not need to live under those conditions assenting to them. We can bear our testimony against whatever we morally disapprove. We can assert our conviction by word or by the silent protest of life that those conditions are not right, and so to live in the midst of conditions in which we do not believe, but from which we cannot escape, is not compromise. It is compromise when we surrender our principles so that others do not understand what those principles are, or when we hold back something that is vital, or cover over deceptively or misleadingly something essential. When we take before men a position that is inconsistent with the position that in our hearts we are taking before God, that is compromise, and that is wrong. Regarding the truth in which we believe, the principles by which we know life ought to be lived, regarding these things there cannot be compromise, in our lives or in the Christian Church.

There is a noble essay by Mr. John Morley, as he once was, on this subject of compromise, its nature and limits, of which Scott Holland says in "Lux Mundi" that "no one can read that book without being either the better or the worse for it." In it Morley takes up three different spheres of life. First, the formation of opinion; second, the expression of opinion when it is called out from us; and, third, the propagation of opinion; and then he pursues this line of argument: In the matter of the formation of opinion there cannot be any compromise at all. Every one of us is bound to hunt for the truth, no matter what the truth may be, and when we have found it, to give our lives absolutely to it. In the realm of the expression of opinion, nobody has any right to deceive any one regarding his principles and convictions when they are called forth. But in the third place, he admits room for compromise when it comes to the aggressive propagation of our convictions. He says that every man is not bound to propagate what he believes, and he takes for example his own case,—that of a man who does not believe in the Bible, who has abandoned the old religious views of his people, but who does not regard it as his duty aggressively to propagate his dissentient convictions.

In his own words his thesis is this:

" In the positive endeavour to realize an opinion, to convert a theory into practice, it may be, and very often is, highly expedient to defer to the prejudices of the majority, to move very slowly, to bow to the conditions of the status quo, to practice the very utmost sobriety, self-restraint, and conciliatoriness. The mere expression of opinion, in the next place, the avowal of dissent from received notions, the refusal to conform to language which implies the acceptance of such notions—this rests on a different footing. Here the reasons for respecting the wishes and sentiments of the majority are far less strong, though, as we shall presently see, such reasons certainly exist, and will weigh with all well-considering men. Finally, in the formation of an opinion as to the abstract preferableness of one course of action over another, or as to the truth or falsehood or right significance of a proposition, the fact that the majority of one's contemporaries lean in the other direction is naught, and no more than dust in the balance. In making up our minds as to what would be the wisest line of policy if it were practicable, we have nothing to do with the circumstance that it is not practicable.   And in settling with ourselves whether propositions purporting to state matters of fact are true or not, we have to consider how far they are conformable to the evidence. We have nothing to do with the comfort and solace which they would be likely to bring to others or ourselves, if they were taken as true."

Now, we cannot but be rather grateful that men, who if they spoke would have to oppose Christianity, take this view and remain silent, and yet that is not our principle.   Believing in Christianity, we believe that it would be wrong and unworthy compromise to conceal it and to refrain from propagating it.   Mr. Morley pre-fixed to his essay Whately's saying, "It makes all the difference in the world whether we put truth in the first place or in the second place." We hold to another word of Whately's also: "If our religion is false, we must change it.   If it is true, we must propagate it."   Notice that Morley is speaking not of his doubts, but of his convic-tions.   There is no obligation of a propaganda of insecurity.   There is an obligation to propa-gate positive truth.   It must, of course, be the truth that I believe.   When I am asked what I believe I must, of course, tell the truth.   But we believe something far more than that.   The re-ligious truth that one believes he must give his life to propagate throughout the world, and it would not make any difference if he were the only man in the world who held that truth, it would still be his duty, if he believed it was the truth and the great and necessary truth of life, to go out single-handed to defend and propagate it. Athanasius is regarded as an impracticable and troublesome type but the progress of the world is often lifted forward a sheer and discernible stage by such uncompromisingness.

Let us set forth some of the reasons why we may believe that there dare not be, in our Christian life and our Christian service, any compromise whatever, either in our searching for the truth, in our utterance of the truth, or in our aggressive and active propagation of the truth throughout the world. This is to put the matter, of course, very broadly and sweepingly. There is a great deal to be said for some of Morley's nice discriminations. But actual life is a very rough and imperative and elemental thing. The difficulty of acting on any body of wary and wavery casuistical principles is enormous. The really workable principle of actual living must be very simple and uncomplicated and direct. The only safe ethical law is " No lie," no lie whatever or under any justification. So also, however crude and blunt the rule may be, " No compromise" is the only practicable right rule. Mr. Morley closed his essay with such a plain word: "It is better to bear the burden of impracticableness, than to stifle conviction and to pare away principle until it becomes mere hollowness and triviality." And in the beginning he wrote: "Our day of small calculations and petty utilities must first pass away; our vision of the true expediencies must reach further and deeper; our resolution to search for the highest verities, to give up all and follow them, must first become the supreme part of ourselves." The loss by compromise to ourselves and others is certain, while its gain is uncertain and problematical.

In the first place, one believes this because compromise makes no contribution to the settlement of the real issue over truth. It is true that all the boundaries between truth and error are not clear and sharply drawn lines. Often there is a gray and misty region between. And much truth is only slowly and gradually won. But the ideal of truth is clearer than the sun and as pure as the character of God. And we have a far richer chance of winning it and all that it brings with it, if we both think and live it uncompromisingly. "The political spirit," says Mr. Morley in noble words, "is the great force in throwing love of truth and accurate reasoning into a secondary place. The evil does not stop here. This achievement has indirectly countenanced the postponement of intellectual methods, and the diminution of the sense of intellectual responsibility, by a school that is anything rather than political. Theology has borrowed, and coloured for her own use, the principles which were first brought into vogue in politics. If in the one field it is the fashion to consider convenience first and truth second, in the other there is a corresponding fashion of placing truth second and emotional comfort first. If there are some who compromise their real opinions, or the chance of reaching truth, for the sake of gain, there are far more who shrink from giving their intelligence free play, for the sake of keeping undisturbed certain luxurious spiritual sensibilities. . . .

" The intelligence is not free in the presence of a mortal fear lest its conclusions should trouble soft tranquillity of spirit. There is always hope of a man so long as he dwells in the region of the direct categorical proposition and the unambiguous term ; so long as he does not deny the rightly drawn conclusions after accepting the major and minor premises. This may seem a scanty virtue and very easy grace. Yet experience shows it to be too hard of attainment for those who tamper with disinterestedness of conviction, for the sake of luxuriating in the softness of spiritual transport without interruption from a syllogism. It is true that there are now and then in life as in history noble and fair natures, that by the silent teaching and unconscious example of their inborn purity, star-like constancy, and great devotion, do carry the world about them to further heights of living than can be attained by ratiocination. But these, the blame-

less and loved saints of the earth, rise too rarely
on our dull horizons to make a rule for the world.
The law of things is that they who tamper with
veracity, from whatever motive, are tampering
with the vital force of human progress. Our
comfort and the delight of the religious imagination are no better than forms of self-indulgence,
when they are secured at the cost of that love of
truth on which, more than on anything else, the
increase of light and happiness among men must
depend. We have to fight and do lifelong battle against the forces of darkness, and anything
that turns the edge of reason blunts the surest
and most potent of our weapons." We do not
believe in compromising, because it makes no
contribution to the larger discerning of truth or
the triumphing of that truth over error.

In the second place, we do not believe in it
because it creates a great many more difficulties
than it removes. Now, Paul was invited to this
compromising course in Jerusalem by his mis-
guided friends because they thought it would
avoid trouble. They wanted to set Paul right
with the Jewish Christians in the city, and maybe
with the Jews who were not Christians; they
wanted to remove an impression which they
thought prevailed regarding Paul's attitude
towards the Mosaic customs in the Gentile
world.

Now, as a matter of fact, the principle of that

impression was true, for although, as **Dr. Mc-Giffert** says, Paul

"recognized the legitimacy of Jewish Christianity, and the right of Peter and other apostles to preach to the Jews the Gospel of circumcision, and though there is no evidence that he ever undertook to lead the Jews as a people to cease observing their ancestral law, he had certainly been in the habit of insisting that his Jewish converts should associate on equal terms with their Gentile brethren, and that they should not allow their law to act in any way as a barrier to the freest and most intimate association with them.   But this, of course, meant, in so far, their violation of the law's commands.   It is certain also that Paul had preached for years the doctrine that not the Gentile Christian alone but the Jewish Christian as well is absolutely free from all obligation to keep the law of Moses, and though such teaching might not always result in a disregard of that law by his Jewish converts, it must have a tendency to produce that effect and doubtless did in many cases.   It is clear therefore that both accusations had much truth in them, and it is difficult to suppose that Paul can have deliberately attempted in Jerusalem to prove them wholly false.

"And yet, though as an honourable man and a man of principle he can hardly have undertaken to demonstrate that there was no truth in the reports which were circulated concerning him, it may well be that he tried to show that they were not wholly true.   It was evidently assumed by those who accused him of 'teaching all the Jews which are among the Gentiles to forsake Moses, telling them not to circumcise their children, neither to walk after the customs,' that he hated the Jewish law and that he was doing all that lay in his power to destroy it ; that he believed

and that he taught everywhere that its observance was under any and all circumstances a positive sin.   But this
assumption was not true.   Paul was certainly not hostile
to the law in any such sense.   He believed that it had no
binding authority over a Christian, and he opposed with
all his might the idea that its observance had any value as
a means of salvation, or that it contributed in any way to
the believer's righteousness or growth in grace ; but he
held no such view of the law as made its observance neces-
sarily sinful, and rendered it impossible for him ever to
observe it himself in any respect.   And it was not at all
unnatural that he should desire to convince the Christians
of Jerusalem of the fact ; especially when he had come
thither with the express purpose of conciliating them and
winning their favour for himself and for his Gentile converts.   He would have been very foolish under these circumstances to allow such a false impression touching his
attitude towards the law to go uncontradicted.'' [1]

This is a satisfactory defense if one were needed
of Paul's course, but no one would question his
motive.   That was right enough and he evidently
acted in all good conscience, but the procedure,
instead of getting him out of his trouble, got him
into worse trouble.   It always does that.   I do not
believe any man was ever permanently helped
by compromise.   Every man who has begun to
play with it has been drawn into worse difficulties and troubles, or has gone down, perhaps
without conscious difficulty but with real moral
loss, to a lower level of life.   For one thing,

[1] '' The Apostolic Age,'' p. 341.

compromise blurs the line of cleavage between truth and error, and that is exactly what no one of us can afford to have done. We do not want the lines of distinction between what is true and what is false slurred over for us. We want them sharpened so that we shall make as little mistake as possible as to where they lie. Furthermore compromise gets us into more difficulty than it removes, because it throws together things that are not congruous or reconcilable. This is its very nature. It brings into one bed things that cannot sleep together, into one union things that cannot be tied. And it postpones real settlements in the interest of spurious arrangements, sacrificing some

"greater good for the less, on no more creditable ground than that the less is nearer. It is better to wait, and to defer the realization of our ideas until we can realize them fully, than to defraud the future by truncating them, if truncate them we must, in order to secure a partial triumph for them in the immediate present. . . . What is the sense, and what is the morality, of postponing the wider utility to the narrower? Nothing is so sure to impoverish an epoch, to deprive conduct of nobleness, and character of elevation."

These are Mr. Morley's closing words. This is the second reason why we believe there can be no room for compromise in our Christian life or service.

In the third place, it encourages evil by mak-

ing it think that having got so much it can get
the rest, and so it prolongs the life of evil. That
is exactly what compromise did in the old days
of slavery. Every one of those early com-
promises prolonged the life of evil which at last
the nation had to pour out its blood to destroy.
That is what compromise always does. It per-
suades evil that, after all, maybe evil can win the
victory, that having gotten so much from us it
can get the rest if only it will be patient, and we
simply increase the courage of our foe in proportion as we make any compromise with him
instead of standing up face to face against him
from the very beginning. And so it destroys the
power and might of right causes by mixing in
the taint of wrong. You do not make a good
man better by putting a dash of bad in him.
You do not make a good cause stronger by letting the evil come in; you only weaken its
strength and power. Compromise plays into
the hands of the very evil which we are here to
overcome and destroy.

In the fourth place, compromise breaks down
the strength of rigid consistency, and by letting
in one qualification prepares the way for others.
That is the reason why it is so much harder for
a man to be a moderate drinker than to be a
total abstainer. As was said of Samuel Johnson,
"He could practice abstinence but not temperance." When a man has made up his mind that

he will never do a thing, it is a great deal easier for him to refuse to do it in any given instance than if he has made up his mind that he will do it moderately, because he never knows when he ceases to be moderate. There is a sharp line between moderate drinking and total abstinence. That boundary line no one can ever mistake, but the boundary line between intemperance and moderation is not located anywhere. There is no definite border between those two countries. As a matter of fact, every man starts in by being a moderate drinker. He never intended to become anything else but a moderate drinker when he began. But there is a boundary line so clear that a blind man can see it between yes and no, between not doing a thing at all and doing that thing only moderately. We believe in the principle of absolutely no compromise in moral habit and principle, and we believe in the same principle in our clear and evangelical convictions regarding the Christian faith.

In the fifth place, we ought to shun all such compromise because it undermines our confidence in men, and the solid unity of their coöperative action. We know where truth is, but we never know where calculating compromise may be. In the language of the deaf and dumb this is the sign for truth—a straight line right away from your mouth—for the simple reason that between two points there is only one straight line, but there may be many crooked lines. The truth is always a single thing, but the error,—no man knows what it may be. No compromise makes possible unity of accord by giving people one standard on which they can rely, and by supplying confidence in the stability of men and their convictions. But we cannot follow the compromising man, for as soon as he gets out of our sight we do not know where he will be.

It is the man who makes no compromise, who stands fast by truth, that we know we can locate. It was that which gave Stonewall Jackson his huge power as a leader of men in the Civil War. He was a man of the most unflinching Christian convictions. He was one who never moved the breadth of a hair from his loyalty to his Lord or to truth as he saw truth in the presence of his Lord. Colonel Henderson draws for us a rich picture of the great soldier's character and it is full of genial and kindly touches, but it is faithful also in its account of the man's rigid and inflexible righteousness.

"Jackson's religion entered into every action of his life. No duty, however trivial, was begun without asking a blessing, or ended without returning thanks. 'He had long cultivated,' he said, ' the habit of connecting the most trivial and customary acts of life with a silent prayer.' He took the Bible as his guide, and it is possible that his literal interpretation of its precepts caused many to regard him as a fanatic. His observance of the Sabbath was hardly in accordance with ordinary usage. He never read a letter on that day, nor posted one ; he believed that the Government in carrying the mails was violating a divine law, and he considered the suppression of such traffic one of the most important duties of the legislature. Such opinions were uncommon, even among the Presbyterians, and his rigid respect for truth served to strengthen the impression that he was morbidly scrupulous. If he unintentionally made a misstatement—even about some trifling matter—as soon as he discovered his mistake he would lose no time and spare no trouble in hastening to correct it. ' Why, in the name of reason,' he was asked, ' do you walk a mile in the rain for a perfectly unimportant thing ? ' ' Simply because I have discovered that it was a misstatement, and I could not sleep comfortably unless I put it right.'

" He had occasion to censure a cadet who had given, as Jackson believed, the wrong solution of a problem. On thinking the matter over at home, he found that the pupil was right and the teacher wrong. It was late at night and in the depth of winter, but he immediately started off to the Institute, some distance from his quarters, and sent for the cadet. The delinquent, answering with much trepidation the untimely summons, found himself to his astonishment the recipient of a frank apology. Jackson's scruples carried him even further. Persons who interlarded their conversation with the unmeaning phrase ' you know ' were often astonished by the blunt interruption that he did *not* know ; and when he was entreated at parties or receptions to break through his dietary rules, and for courtesy's sake to seem to accept some delicacy, he would always refuse with the reply that he had ' no genius for seeming.' But if he carried his conscientiousness to extremes, if he laid down stringent rules for his own governance, he neither set himself up for a model nor did he attempt to force his convictions upon others.   He was always tolerant; he knew his own faults, and his own temptations, and if he could say nothing good of a man he would not speak of him at all.   But he was by no means disposed to overlook conduct of which he disapproved, and undue leniency was a weakness to which he never yielded.   If he once lost confidence or discovered deception on the part of one he trusted, he withdrew himself as far as possible from any further dealings with him; and whether with the cadets or with his brother-officers, if an offense had been committed of which he was called upon to take notice, he was absolutely inflexible.   Punishment or report inevitably followed.   No excuses, no personal feelings, no appeals to the suffering which might be brought upon the innocent, were permitted to interfere with the execution of his duty."

" As exact as the multiplication table," some one said of him, "and as full of things military as an arsenal."   Those of us who are looking for the secret of Christian influence over others may be sure that we will find it here.   Men are not going to follow the shifting man.   They will follow the man who makes no compromise, who has his firm convictions and who stands by those convictions, no matter what the cost of his loyalty may be. Recent American politics are rather eloquent and convincing on this point.

In the sixth place, compromise in principle substitutes reliance upon majorities for reliance upon the truth, and the majorities never have been right and we may doubt whether, until our Lord Jesus Christ comes again, they ever will be right. God never has relied upon the majority. He never has waited to do His work until it was ready to side with Him. In all ages God has done His work by the few. In Old Testament times He did it by the few. The one principle prevailed always—not by might, nor by power. It was ever only "the Sword of the Lord and of Gideon." When our Lord came He did His work with the few. Through all the ages God has been working so, and we simply depart from His whole method in history when by compromise we try to get the force of the majority on our side. The force of the majority does not amount to anything in comparison with the force of truth. "The history of success," says Mr. Morley, "as we can never too often repeat to ourselves, is the history of minorities." And we do not believe in compromise because it substitutes our reliance upon the majority for our reliance upon the truth of God, and upon the strength of God to enable the few with the truth to triumph against the error of the crowd. This passes for foolish idealism and some of our most popular political leaders and reformers have poured scorn upon the idealists and dreamers, who are not to be numbered among the practical men.

"One would like to ask them what purpose is served by an ideal, if it is not to make a guide for practice and a landmark in dealing with the real. A man's loftiest and most ideal notions must be of a singularly ethereal and, shall we not say, senseless kind, if he can never see how to take a single step that may tend in the slightest degree towards making them more real. If an ideal has no point of contact with what exists, it is probably not much more than the vapid outcome of intellectual or spiritual self-indulgence. If it has such a point of contact, then there is sure to be something which a man can do towards the fulfillment of his hopes. He cannot substitute a new national religion for the old, but he can at least do something to prevent people from supposing that the adherents of the old are more numerous than they really are, and something to show them that good ideas are not all exhausted by the ancient forms. He cannot transform a monarchy into a republic, but he can make sure that one citizen at least shall aim at republican virtues, and abstain from the debasing complaisance of the crowd." [1]

And we might add, "he cannot instantly make truth the life of the nation, but he can be loyal to its commandments. He cannot make political leaders honest and patriotic, but he can refuse to profit by their dishonesty or to regard them as honest men if they will but wear his badge and seek their own ends by promoting his. He can form his own ideals of honour and glory and live by them whatever way others may go."

In the seventh place, compromise increases in peril as we draw near the highest. If you take a man who is down on the lower levels, com-

[1] Morley, " Compromise," p. 226.

promise does not mean as much to him as it does to men who have been climbing up. The nearer we come to Christ and the highest truth, the more perilous does compromise become. As Edward Thring said: "In proportion to excellence, compromise is impossible. A single leak sinks a great ship, a raft that is all leaks floats." That is just the deep lesson that men and women need to learn; that the higher and cleaner and more morally lofty or exacting the life, the more perilous compromise becomes to it. One has heard Christian men say sometimes that they thought they were safe in doing what this or that man, not as strong or experienced or mature, could do. It is a great mistake. The clearer and stronger a man's life, the more careful must the man be, the more solicitous, the more anxious, lest thinking he stands he falls. One of the greatest things about the life of Paul was the humility and self-distrust in which he walked, fearing lest when he had preached to others he himself might be a castaway. We have to learn that here lies power and duty, and that the cleaner Christ makes any human life, the more careful must that life be to keep all its habits pure and unsullied, and its convictions of truth unflinching and firm.

It was this principle that made our friend, S. H. Hadley, and that makes so many men who have escaped from the slavery of drink, go to extremes in cutting off physical indulgences. Mr. Hadley not only dropped once and forever the use of alcohol, but he stopped tobacco too, and he tried to get every drunkard whom he was seeking to save to discontinue the use of nicotine. He held that men should be clean every whit and his strong conviction was that while he would not for a moment class such indulgences together, nevertheless the man who wanted to be free from the one would find his deliverance far easier if he sloughed off the other also. It is safer and easier to be thoroughgoing and indiscriminate, if you will, than to be always calculating how great risks can be safely run.

And, lastly, we believe in no compromise because the truth is bound to prevail, and it will triumph the soonest when it is least hampered and tied up with error or with qualification. One might stop here to make a defense on this ground of the fanatics and devotees, but it is enough to say that the truth is going to prevail because it is God's truth, and hell and all hell's power in the world cannot stand against it. What is the use in delaying the day of that triumph by compromising with error? The right will prevail all the faster if we make no compromise with error, if we go out and preach unflinchingly and courageously with no compromise, with no surrender or economy or adaptations, the hard, plain truth of God as we see

it. If what we think is truth is really error, it
will be the sooner beaten down for being made
to stand up for itself. But if it is indeed the
truth we know it will prevail the more in the
world as we keep it free from all connection with
anything that will weaken or becloud it.

I know how much danger there is in such an
attitude as this if we take it up towards the truth
that we hold. It lies in our human nature to go
to violence or extremes with everything. Martin
Luther used to say that human nature is like a
drunken man trying to ride a horse, you prop
him up on one side and he topples over on the
other. It is that way with us. We try to be
firm and we become hard-hearted. We pride
ourselves on uncompromising loyalty to the
truth and we lack the tenderness and sympathy.
Moreover, as Bushnell said in his essay on
" Christian Comprehensiveness " :

"It is the common infirmity of mere human reformers
that, when they rise up to cast out an error, it is generally
not till they have kindled their passions against it. If they
begin with reason, they are commonly moved, in the last
degree, by their animosities instead of reason. And as
animosities are blind, they, of course, see nothing to respect, nothing to spare. The question whether possibly
there may not be some truth or good in the error assailed,
which is needed to qualify and save the equilibrium of
their own opposing truth, is not once entertained. Hence
it is that men, in expelling one error, are perpetually

thrusting themselves into another, as if unwilling or unable to hold more than half the truth at once."

And yet these dangers are lesser dangers than the danger of surrendering the truth. And we can be guarded from them by the great and unselfish love that guarded Paul. The man who loves others more than he loves himself, who holds human lives sacred and free from invasion, who is seeking not his own glory, but the glory of God and the good of men, is in little danger from an absolutely uncompromising loyalty to the truth.

And if ever men have any doubts or misgivings regarding this, or if the time of discouragements and fears comes to them, and they look with longing to the multitudes who act together, while they think of themselves as just a few, bearing testimony for the truth against error and sin, they may encourage themselves with Mr. Matthew Arnold's doctrine of the remnant, or better yet, by remembering the great Solitary, Jesus Christ. How lonesomely He walked His way; seeing what no other soul was seeing; standing alone for the great truth which He uttered, and at last meeting death upon the cross alone; one of His disciples having betrayed Him, another having three times denied that he ever knew Him, and all the others having left Him and gone away! And yet as we look back, we see that lonely cross ruling the whole world, and that forsaken figure men are clothing now with the crown of everlasting light, and His name is above every name. All that we are asked to do is simply to follow in His train, to take up the truth which He opened, and for that truth to be willing to live, and, which is far easier, if need be, to die. Our lives are ours for this one thing, that through them, without compromise with error or with sin, God may bear testimony to Himself, and whether He does that through many years or through few, through peaceful personal service or through storm and tragedy, is of no consequence. The one thing that is of consequence is that we should know and be true to God.

But there is a better way to set forth and commend this principle as a law of life than by arguing it in these general terms. Let the principle put on flesh and live before us in a man :

"And Elijah the Tishbite, who was of the sojourners of Gilead, said unto Ahab, As the Lord, the God of Israel, liveth, before whom I stand, there shall not be dew nor rain these years, but according to my word."

The old man who spoke these words was one of the four great characters of the Old Testament. He and Moses and Samuel and David stood apart in the thought of the Hebrew people. Indeed, there was a sense in which he and Moses were in a class by themselves. The appearance of those two with our Lord on the Mountain of

Transfiguration was only an illustration of the place which they held in the imagination of Israel.

These were the first words he spoke as he bursts on our view. What lay behind them we can only surmise. He was a Tishbite, one " of the sojourners of Gilead," dwelling beyond the Jordan, a man brought up in the desert. There on the level sands, with the eye of God looking down upon him, he had come to a deep feeling of the soul's lonely stand before God, and convinced of God and the righteousness of God he came over the Jordan to speak his message and do his work in the organized national life of his people. He was a clean-limbed, frugal-lived man, who gathered up his skirts about him, we are told, and ran straight away sixteen miles before the chariot of Ahab, from Carmel to the entering in of Jezreel; a calm, quiet, courageous, firm-principled man; bred so in the desert with God.

We do not have any very elaborate story of his life. He appears on the stage and then he vanishes. There are long periods of time covering years when he disappears entirely from the record. We can condense what we know about his life into six brief chapters, between each two of which there is an interval, in some cases, a long interval of time.

He appears first of all in connection with the

great drought which he prophesied and which lasted for the three years he had foretold. We see him by the little brook Cherith, fed of the ravens, until through the long cessation of the rain the brook itself disappeared. Then we see him in the house of the widow of Sarepta, feeding with her on her little supply of meal, and in her hour of depthless sorrow raising her son from death to life. And then, in the second chapter, he breaks forth once more upon the national stage. Ahab and Obadiah, his chief man, had sought for him up and down the land, having divided the country between them, partly that they might seek water for their fast diminishing herds, partly that they might meet again and punish this troubler of Israel. At last, on one of the highways, the man of God appeared to the prime minister and told him that he had no fear to meet the king and would do so if he would carry word to Ahab. True to his word, he met the king, confronted him with his disloyalty to Jehovah, and challenged him to produce the prophets of Baal for the great test on Mount Carmel; and then, after his triumph, Elijah again disappears.

In the third chapter we have the only account of the man's inner life. If it were not for that chapter with its story of his subjective struggle, Elijah would be no example for us men of this day. In all the other chapters of the story he appears absolutely undaunted, unafraid of the face of man, clearly convinced of what God would have him do, and absolutely fearless in the doing of it. But here we are shown the man in his own inward wavering, in doubt in some measure about the reality or power of his mission, afraid to carry forward that which he had set out to do with such daring spirit ; and in the wilderness alone, first beneath the juniper tree and then on Mount Horeb, Elijah had to face again his life and settle himself once more in that faith in the living God which had brought him out of the desert. And God stood out and spoke to him, and Elijah rose up on his feet once more a man unafraid to resume his mission. God bade him return and anoint a new king over Syria and a new king over Israel, and to go to Abel-meholah and find his own successor, the young man Elisha, plowing behind his oxen. And the prophet went out from his hour of discouragement to find at once the young man who was to take up his work after him and to be an even mightier prophet than he.

Then for a long time Elijah disappears again, only to reappear when he confronts Ahab once more, in Naboth's vineyard, shows him how little he fears him, and pronounces upon him the judgment of Jehovah. Then he vanishes from the stage for three years at least of solitary meditation in the wilderness, vanishes so long that the common people apparently forgot him, so that when one day he met a little party of the servants of the new king Ahaziah on the highway bound to Ekron to consult Baal-zebub, they did not know who the prophet was and brought back his message to the king, able only to say of him that he was a hairy man, with a leather girdle about his loins. But the king well knew that the Tishbite had broken once more upon the stage of the nation's life, and he bowed beneath the judgments of God that the man from Gilead denounced.

Then in the concluding chapter we see Elijah and his young man coming down from Gilgal to Bethel and then to Jericho and then back to the wilderness out of which he had come, that from his own deserts where he had come to know God he might go back to God again. And there in the chariot of fire the man who was himself "the chariots of Israel, and the horsemen thereof," went up to the Lord God of Israel, Who was alive, to meet Him before Whom he had always stood.

One does not wonder that the old man impressed as he did the imagination of his people, and that when centuries later John the Baptist emerged upon the stage challenging the attention of the nation, almost the first question addressed to him was, " Art thou Elijah ? "

And we have the secret of Elijah's life given

to us in these words with which he is introduced to us, " As the LORD God of Israel liveth, before whom I stand." Out there in the barrenness of the desert beyond the Jordan, Elijah had come to believe in a God Who was alive, and before Whom he lived his life. The deserts have never bred polytheism. The great polytheistic systems have sprung from the lush jungles of the tropics. The great monotheisms have been born in the deserts. And out on the lonely sands beyond the Jordan, beyond the hills and amid the great level places where there was no one but God, Elijah came to know that He was and to know that his life stood in Him.

This was the principle of the man's life—the consuming conviction of a living God and of the commission of His uncompromising service. Indeed we are not sure that we know Elijah's name. It is possible that the name by which we think we know him is only a pseudonym—Elijah, " My God is Jehovah." It may be that from the very repetition of this phrase to which he was addicted, " The LORD God of Israel, before whom I stand," men came at last to call him by the opening note of his message, " the man of the living God."

Now what that message meant to Elijah was just this : that the Lord God was no dead force, no unknown cause of things, that the Lord God was alive, and that a man was to have dealings

with Him ; that a man's life was not his own
personal and irresponsible experiment, but a
work to be done in front of God ; and that a man
must reckon in all his thoughts, in all his ways,
with One Who lives, and go out and do his work
in the world in the consciousness of his relationship and his subjection to an active, working,
personal God Who would stand by him in the
fire, would uphold him before kings, and carry
him through to the end of each of his appointed
tasks.   If there is one thing that we need to get
clearly fixed in our own lives it is the matter of
our attitude towards this infinite and unseen God
Who is alive.

This faith in a God Who is alive, before
Whose face a man is to live his life, is no mere
theory.   You cannot find any conviction that
will more really mould and transform all our
conduct and put uncompromising stiffness in it
than the conviction that we are living our lives
thus before the eyes of a God Who observes.
In the life of Thring of Uppingham we are told
of an incident that pleased him greatly.   It is a
story that came to him regarding a little group
of boys who were spending the summer in
France.   A visitor saw these English schoolboys
and overheard their conversation as to what they
should do on Sunday.   Some of the boys were
proposing a certain course of action, and all
seemed to agree until one fellow spoke up and

said: "No, I do not agree.   I will not do it."   And
when the other lads urged him to come along,
he still insisted that he would not.   They asked
him his reasons.   He said: " Well, Thring would
not like it, and what Thring would not like I do
not intend to do."   " Well, but Thring isn't
here," they said; " he's back at Uppingham."
" I do not care," said the boy; " Thring would
not like it."   He believed that he was living in
a real sense—I mean in the most real sense of
all, in the life of his personal will—before the
standards of his master, and by those standards
as in the light of his master's countenance he insisted that he would uncompromisingly live.
Before the eyes of God a man will beware how
he lives his life.   If he knows that this life of his
can find no darkness where he can hide himself
from God, if he knows that all of his days are to
be spent before His face, that all his deeds are to
be done beneath the gaze of God, assuredly
that will govern and control a man's decisions
about his practical ways.   The consciousness of
a living God will give direction to a man's moral
life.

And it will not only give direction.   There is
many a man among us who knows that the consciousness of a God Who is alive not only gives
determination and direction to his ways, but puts
a new power and inspiration in them.

A friend in New York tells a lovely story

about a boy in one of the great English schools. He was an only child, and his mother died when he was but a little fellow. Between him and his father there grew up relations of the most delicate and sensitive intimacy. The father was blind, so that the little boy had to be his father's eyes, and until the day came when the lad had to go away to school there was scarcely an hour when the two were separated. But at last the time came and the boy went. He became the best athlete in his school. One spring, just before the final game in which the boy was to bowl for his own school, tidings came that his father was seriously ill and he must come home. The news sent the whole school into lamentation, for they were afraid that he might not recover and that if he did not the boy could not play in the concluding and critical game. And indeed, as it turned out, the father died. The day before the game was to be played the boy came back to school, and, to the amazement of all, let it be known that he intended to play. The next day he took his place and played as he had never played in his life before. When at last the game was over and the school had won its triumph, one of the masters came to the boy and expressed to him the delighted surprise of the school at what he had done and their amazement both that he had played at all and at the way he had played. "Why," said the boy, "didn't you understand? I wouldn't have missed it for anything. That was the first game my father ever saw me play." Beneath the consciousness that for the first time his father's eyes were open and watching him the boy had discovered capacities of power that he hardly knew he possessed before. Beneath the eye of our Father, Who is looking upon the game that we are playing, where is the man that cannot play a better game, who cannot draw on the reservoirs of power untouched before, who cannot come out and do his work in the world and live his life with larger inspiration and strength, with more dominion and sovereignty, because he is living it before a God Who is alive? To such a man will compromise not seem a filial insult impossible except by a base degradation of the soul?

And not only did Elijah's principle determine his conduct and pour inspiration into it; it was this principle of a God Who is alive that made him absolutely fearless. He was not only unafraid of physical harm, but he had none of that subtler fear that every man knows—the fear that he himself will fail, the fear that he cannot carry himself safely through. What you and I are afraid of is not the things that are without; our enemy is inside. Treachery within the walls is all that we need to dread, and our deepest fear is of our own failure. That was the great thing in Elijah's life, that he dared to stand on Mount Carmel, before all that crowd of priests, confident and fearless. He knew he would prevail, that he had not promised in vain that God would answer. The man who knows that he is living his life before a God Who is alive and doing his work in the name of a God Who is alive is not afraid either of what men can do to him or of the failure that he may make himself.

There is a story in the life of Dr. Schauffler that illustrates how to-day too men can rise into just such fearlessness. The missionaries were being bothered a great deal in Constantinople by Russian machinations against the Protestant missions in the empire, and Dr. Schauffler went to see the Russian ambassador. "I might as well tell you now, Mr. Schauffler," said the ambassador, "that the Emperor of Russia, who is my master, will never allow Protestantism to set its foot in Turkey." The old missionary looked at him for a moment and then replied: "Your Excellency, the kingdom of Christ, who is my Master, will never ask the Emperor of all the Russias where it may set its foot." And he went on with his mission unintimidated by any agencies working in the dark against him, because he was confident that the living God Whose work he was doing would achieve for him His own victory.

And we see in this story of Elijah another

thing that this great conviction will do for a man : it will make a troubler of him. " Art thou he," said Ahab when he met Elijah in the midst of the great famine, " art thou he that troubleth Israel ? " " No," said Elijah ; " thou art he who troubles Israel." And yet they were both troubling Israel, the one with the iniquities into which he was leading the people, the other because the principle of the living God dominating his life drove him as a great moral force against the evils of his time. A man cannot live in a college or university with a faith that God is living and that he himself is living in front of God, and be quiet before the moral iniquities and evils he will find. It is not enough for a man to say, " I will simply be myself, live my own clean life, and let my silent influence count." If his silent influence does not count, no other influence of his will count. But the silence is not enough. A little while ago I copied from one of the letters of Mandel Creighton, late Bishop of London, written to his boys who were away at school, this bit of advice. " You will see, then," he writes to one son, who had just been made a monitor in his school, " you will see, then, that the chief influence of a monitor is in his example. But this is the point on which I have seen many people deceive themselves. They trust to what they call the force of silent example. That is most pernicious. If you content yourself with merely keeping school rules and doing what is right yourself and keeping out of the way of any fellows who you know are doing wrong, or if you stand by and listen to them saying what they ought not, without reproof, you are doing wrong. No, that won't do. It is part of the essence of good to fight against evil. You must set your face strongly against all that is bad, and must put down not only all that you find in the course of your walk, but you must go out of your walk to find it in order to put it down."

There has been much complaint these last years because in high places in this land there have been men who were troublers of the nation. The great need of the nation has been men who were prepared to make trouble in order that, at last, righteousness might come. Things that have thought themselves secure will be shaken ; long vested interests that have believed themselves to be sacred will have their sanctity scrutinized ; and men will come at last into their rights and their righteousness, if we are prepared, following the old Tishbite, to live our lives before the God Who is alive.

And this same principle brings peace and quiet and tranquillity to men. Elijah shook once, we know, but only once. Every time we see him on the public stage, no matter whom he is confronting—Jezebel, Ahab, Obadiah, Ahaziah —he is standing with confident soul, quiet and still. We can be sure that if on that day at Mount Carmel we could have first mingled with those four hundred and fifty priests of Baal who knew that their day of doom had come, and then have gone over and stood by the side of the old man, we should have found the old man the most quiet and placid person on the mountainside and his heart beat the calmest. And we may be sure that we can go in the same tranquillity and calm and steadfastness in which the old Tishbite lived, if we will believe as deeply as he did in a Lord God Who is alive, and will live our lives before His face with as little compromise and fear.

And it is a great conviction like this of Elijah's that steadies men in the hour of their trial and that when they fall redeems them again. The old prophet fell down. He ran from a woman's threats, and beneath the juniper tree and then on Horeb, he shook and was afraid. But God, Who was alive before, was alive still, and He came to Mount Horeb, where the man lay in his spiritual petulance and fear, and He was not in the great wind, and He was not in the great earthquake, and He was not in the great fire, but at last in the still small voice of life He spoke to Elijah, and Elijah rose up on his feet once more and went out to complete his work in unfaltering triumph.

It works that way still. There is a letter of

Abraham Lincoln, the original of which is preserved in the state capitol at Albany.   It is a letter Lincoln wrote granting a pardon to a deserter.

ExECUTIVE MANSION,
WASHINGTON, October 4, 1864.

Upon condition that Roswell McIntyre of Company E, Sixth Regiment of New York Cavalry, returns to his regiment and faithfully serves out his term, making up for lost time, or until otherwise lawfully discharged, he is fully pardoned for any supposed desertion heretofore committed ; and this paper is his pass to go to his regiment.

ABRAHAM LINCOLN.

On the side of it is indorsed : "Quartermaster's Office, New York City, October 22, 1864. Transportation furnished to Baltimore, Maryland.   H. Brownson"; and at the bottom in a different hand is this indorsement : "Taken from the body of R. McIntyre at the Battle of Five Forks, Virginia, 1865."   So he went back and died like a man, with his pardon on his person. And to-day, to the coward and the deserter and the traitor, the man who has compromised and the man who has run away, the same Lord God Who set Elijah on his feet is speaking, and He is able to send him back to be faithful, even unto death.   Thanks be to a God Who does not compromise and Who is still alive.

LECTURE V

THE LIFE INVISIBLE

IT is interesting to note two contrary tendencies in the current appraisal of spiritual values in America. On the one hand there is what has been called, not altogether happily, the tendency of ethical materialism. In its best form it is simply a demand for reality, the renewal of the old words, "By their fruits ye shall know them." "Show me thy faith by thy works." In its less worthy forms it is the effort to eliminate spiritual expression and formal religion from areas of life where these have been most familiar. Illustrations in extreme forms abound.

We are told now that in charity love has nothing to do with the matter, that the introduction of religious sentiment is only mischievous and misleading, that the issue is one purely of proper economic principle and organization. It is a question of employment for the unemployed, or of calculating accurately the amount of need, counting the hungry mouths and fixing the quantity of bread, and then determining scientifically how much of the bread the hungry should earn, and how much society through appropriate and unsentimental machinery should supply.

In medical philanthropy the new idea is that ideas have nothing to do with it. The good Samaritan, we are told, did not give the wounded man a tract or say anything to him about the religious views or motives of his benefactor. He was satisfied to heal his skin and stop at that. Let the chaplains depart from the hospitals.

And so also in social service. The legitimate work is to improve the culinary methods of the neighbourhood, to provide innocent games and sports, to secure more adequate food supplies for living bodies and to assist in the burial of dead ones ; but Christ must not be mentioned, and religious issues must not be raised.

These are extreme illustrations, but they are perfectly familiar, and the tendency they represent is indisputable. In this view our Lord, of course, was far astray when He talked to His disciples by Jacob's well about having meat to eat which they knew not. " Meat ! " say our modern ethical materialists. " Meat is meat— beef or bread. It is not a metaphor. Meat that is a metaphor is a mockery." Well, it would be if it were offered for food to a hungry man, but it is not a mockery to the man who would go hungry to feed the hungry. And the whole modern question is not between those who would give real meat to the hungry and those who would give only metaphorical meat. It is between those who want to deal with people's skins only and those who mean to deal both with their skins and with their souls, between those who conceive of man as mainly belly and back and those to whom our real life is the life invisible.

It is a very curious phenomenon, this exclusion of Christian ideas from the very area which they created. For all this charity and philanthropy and social service were produced by the ideas of Christianity. And now the fruit says to the vine and to the inward life, "I have no need of thee." Of course not all the fruit says this. Some of it only says, "Vine and inward life, there is a prejudice against you. You would do well to conceal yourself. I will pretend to be the real thing." But some of the fruit has gone further. "I am the real thing," it says. "I know more than James. Faith must not only show works : works are faith. There is no need of metaphysics or creeds. Deeds are religion. The only wealth is tangible wealth, things handled, works seen, bread out of the ground, not down from heaven. Meat that the disciples could not see is too pallid for this earth. Man is his skin and the bag which it contains, and religion must understand this."

At the same time that this suicidal tendency is operating in the field of man's highest values seeking to destroy his standards and to discredit the title-deeds of all his greatest treasures, a precisely contrary tendency is acting in commerce and politics, in the field of man's lower values. While men are busy on the one hand in the effort to materialize the spiritual wealth which Christianity has produced, other men are seeking with a new earnestness to spiritualize our material wealth. As education, science, philanthropy, surrenders the spiritual vision and ideal, trade and politics clutch after it. Never before in the history of the world has there been such an effort as there is to-day to idealize nationalism, to build up spiritual conceptions behind the State, to make racial feeling a religion. If some men think that religious values and spiritual ideas and so-called "metaphysical" notions can be spared from charity and social service, other men are striving with all their might to secure all this rejected mass of vitality and power for patriotism and the national life.

And the same spiritualizing and idealizing tendency is even more evident in commerce and finance. Wealth becomes less and less material. In primitive times riches consisted in flocks and herds and land and in actual gold and silver bullion or coins which their owner put in a crock and buried in his house. Now wealth consists in credit and securities, in figures written on a ledger in a bank, or in scraps of paper in a tin box. The world's work is done with little visible

wealth.   Our new banking system is meant for
this very purpose, to provide immaterial instru-
mentalities.   Millions of dollars are transported
invisibly.   By a cable message or a message
through the air untold wealth that was in London
can be made to appear in New York.   And all
these intangible forms of wealth are exceeded in
the judgment of the late Mr. J. P. Morgan by the
credit of character, something still more "metaphysical."   The spiritualization of the material
keeps pace on one side with the materialization
of the spiritual on the other.

However clear or foggy our ideas on these
issues may be now, viewing them as present
issues, we cannot fail to see sharply the indisputable facts of the past.   Looking backward
we simply do not discern and cannot remember
the visible and outward values or possessors of
values at all.   Where is the actual material
wealth of earlier days, the flocks, the gold and
silver, the palaces?   The amazing thing is that
it is all gone.   The gold and silver which Rome
gathered from the world, which went home to
Spain in the days of the Conquistadores, where is
it all now?   Where are those who boasted it and
built their fame or power on it?   Shelley tells us
in his sonnet, "Ozymandias,"

> " I met a traveller from an antique land
>   Who said, 'Two vast and trunkless legs of stone
>   Stand in the desert.   Near them, on the sand

Half sunk, a shattered visage lies, whose frown
And wrinkled lip, and sneer of cold command
Tell that its sculptor well those passions read
Which yet survive, stamped on those lifeless things,
The hand that mocked them and the heart that fed :
And on the pedestal these words appear :
" My name is Ozymandias, king of kings,
Look on my works, ye Mighty, and despair ! "
Nothing beside remains.   Round the decay
Of that colossal wreck, boundless and bare,
The lone and level sands stretch far away.' "

And what befell Ozymandias' image has befallen almost all the works of the ancients' hands. A few of their temples remain, and the arches of their viaducts and some of the images of their public worship and of their national ideals.   But their wealth and the treasure houses which they kept it in and the palaces of their pleasure and the cities of their pride are gone. I never felt more keenly the tragedy and the truth of this utter transitoriness and insecurity of all national glory than looking over the massive ruins of the palace of the Chosroes kings at Kasr-i-Shirin.   All of Browning's "Love Among the Ruins" seemed to be there in mute evidence before one's eyes :

" Where the quiet-coloured end of evening smiles
            Miles and miles
   On the solitary pastures where our sheep
            Half-asleep
   Tinkle homeward through the twilight, stray or stop
            As they crop —

Was the site once of a city great and gay,
  (So they say)
Of our country's very capital, its prince
  Ages since
Held his court in, gathered councils, wielding far
  Peace or war.

" Now,—the country does not even boast a tree,
  As you see,
To distinguish slopes of verdure, certain rills
  From the hills
Intersect and give a name to, (else they run
  Into one,)
Where the domed and daring palace shot its spires
  Up like fires
O'er the hundred-gated circuit of a wall
  Bounding all,
Made of marble, men might march on nor be pressed,
  Twelve abreast.

" And such plenty and perfection, see, of grass
  Never was !
Such a carpet as, this summer-time, o'erspreads
  And embeds
Every vestige of the city, guessed alone,
  Stock or stone —
Where a multitude of men breathed joy and woe
  Long ago ;
Lust of glory pricked their hearts up, dread of shame
  Struck them tame ;
And that glory and that shame alike, the gold
  Bought and sold.

" Now,—the single little turret that remains
  On the plains,
By the caper overrooted, by the gourd
  Overscored,
While the patching houseleek's head of blossom winks
  Through the chinks —
Marks the basement whence a tower in ancient time
  Sprang sublime.

And a burning ring, all round, the chariots traced
  As they raced,
And the monarch and his minions and his dames
  Viewed the games."

All this is gone.   The only wealth of the past
which has survived is such as Christ referred to.
"I have meat to eat that ye know not of."   The
ideas and the literature which enshrined them
alone remain.   Not the manuscripts.   They are
gone, as though God would show in the most
vivid way His scorn of the visible and earth's
"real."   Not one original page of Plato exists.
But Plato's mind is here still.   The kings are
gone.   But Isaiah and Jeremiah, the men of the
inward resources, spokesmen and ministers of the
invisible life, abide.

> " The tumult and the shouting dies
> The captains and the kings depart
> Still stands Thine against sacrifice
> A humble and a contrite heart."

And the issue is clear enough when we look at
it concretely to-day and contrast the men who
have the inward resources with those who have
not, the movements which are fed from deep
ideal springs with those which deal skin-deep
only with humanity.   In one of our American
cities the president of a large institution was
shelved in the prime of life by younger and less
conservative men who acquired control of the
business.   They treated the older man well, gave

him the nominal headship with his former salary, but really transferred all the power to other men. It was the chance of a lifetime for the older man. He had his strength and his time for any service or ministry or pleasure he might choose. But the only meat which he had to eat was the management of the business, and accordingly he starved to death in a fine home and with a large salary. All that the bag of his body needed he had, but man cannot live by bread alone without a word from God. The Tinker of Bedford Jail heard the key turn in the lock behind him. And did he famish alone? He opened the gate of his house within and out they came—Christian and Great-Heart and Hopeful and Evangelist and Mercy and Dare-to-Die—and the loneliness of John Bunyan's cell became the greatest society on earth, and the immortals who marched out of the wealth of his soul are the companions of millions who could not name one human being who was Bunyan's contemporary. The rich men who have transmitted real wealth have been the lovers, the dreamers, the servers who ate bread at God's hands and who knew and taught men that the life is more than meat and the body than raiment. "She was not daily bread," wrote her niece of Emily Dickinson. "She was star dust."

This above all was characteristic of Christ. Part of our Lord's preëminence of nature and of achievement was the untold wealth of His inward resources. No philanthropist or social worker ever lived who was His equal in all that our ethical materialists admire and praise. But behind all this and as explaining all this He had meat to eat that men knew not, thoughts of God, ideas of origin and destiny, of whence He came and whither He was going, fellowship, purposes, a spiritual program. His wealth was an inward, a communicable and eternal treasure. It nourished Him and was for all men.

"I have meat to eat," said He. "Who brought it to Him?" asked they. "A primrose by the river's brim a yellow primrose" was to them; and it was nothing more. Meat was meat, mutton or beef to His disciples. But to Him the primrose was a volume of revelation. Meat was very life of God within His soul. Language to Christ was windows into the wealth of the eternities and the infinites. To men it was words. His discernment of latent values in men made Him a rich man wherever He found a fellow. He had cargoes of redeemable character afloat on the wide waters of mankind, and these He was forever drawing home. Men brought Him a sinner, flotsam of Galilee; and Jesus saw Himself rich with the latent life of Peter of Pentecost, victor of the gates of hell. The stained hand of the Samaritan concubine became under His faith purified to bear the chalice of the life of God. He had more wealth latent in human character

than Crœsus ever dreamed of.   His universalism,
also, made Him rich with all the wealth of humanity.   All around Him men choked and died
in the stifling air of racial exclusion and prejudice.   He lived in the whole free world.   Thinking in terms of all mankind and all the ages
makes the thinker rich beyond all the dreams of
any racial avarice or national pride.

But above all His meat was simply this : to
walk with God, to do the will of God and to accomplish His work.   His life was in God's will,
His strength in God's companionship.   He lived
powerfully among men because He dwelt deeply
in God.   His wealth was not herds and gold, nor
bonds and credits, nor deeds ; but the power to
do deeds in the might and pity of God.

And the inward resources of Christ which are
true wealth are accessible also to us ; and not accessible only, but indispensable.   We need not
set much store by what the world calls wealth.
Its one worthy use is as capital for human service ;
and Christ who had none of it here still did and
inspired more service than all the world's capital
has performed.   Louis Pasteur was living on a
salary of a few hundred francs.   All that he did
was to examine with a microscope things infin-
itesimally small and to reflect upon them, and
then in his laboratory to write down and send
forth some new ideas.   The practical men derided
his " pure science,"—a mere student of theories,

spinner of silk dreams thinner than the filaments of the silkworms of southern France. But Pasteur's thoughts were the richest source of wealth in France. " Pasteur's discoveries alone," said Huxley, " would suffice to cover the war indemnity paid by France to Germany in 1870." [1] True wealth is inward resources, the love of God's world, of truth and holy thoughts, friendship with the living and the dead, the possession of the Son of God and His words which are spirit and life, and of His Spirit " whom the world cannot receive; for it beholdeth Him not, neither knoweth Him; ye know Him; for He abideth with you, and shall be in you."

And all this wealth may be ours without going anywhere for it. No man brought it to Him. " I have meat," He said. So He calls us to be rich. We do not need to go anywhere for it. No man needs to bring it to us. It is here. It is Himself—the Bread of Life. Can we also say, " I have it—meat to eat, of the world unknown, within my soul, within my soul "?

To be able to say that is our great American need. I will not say that it is a greater need now than it has ever been because we have deteriorated and need to recover the element of spiritual idealism in our national character. We have not deteriorated. Doubtless we have lost many things that it would have been well for us

1 Vallery-Radot, " Life of Pasteur," popular edition, p. 374.

to have kept, and have kept much that it would have been better to lose. But we have gained in our perception of the higher values and we seek them more and not less than ever before. We are far from being what we ought to be, but the past was farther, and we only think otherwise because we clothe the past in mists of idealization. That very error is proof of our deeper spiritual discerning. Evils are challenged now which passed uncondemned a half generation ago. But though we have gained, we need to gain more, and what we need to gain is not something æsthetic or intellectual only, not broader philosophies or wider social programs, not anything external or merely ethical, but something biological and dynamic. We need the push and power of what One and One only offers. "The thief cometh not," said Christ, "but that he may steal, and kill, and destroy: I came that they may have life, and may have it abundantly."

Not long before his death, as all remember, the late Mr. Morgan was summoned to testify before a congressional committee which was seeking to locate the seat of the money power. The object of those examining Mr. Morgan was to bring out the extent of his own influence and control, and to show, if possible, that in the hands of a few men was concentrated the real domination of the financial life of America. The popular impression, after the examination was over, was that Mr. Morgan's modest disavowals were justified by all the testimony, and that there was no one person, or any group of individuals, in this country who possessed so much power as was supposed to reside in the hands of a little company of men.

Now, at the best, there was no question of creating or producing anything. Nobody thought of asking Mr. Morgan whether he could create a grain of wheat, or heal a disease, or bring into existence anything that was not already here. The main question was how much of something that was here already was he, or any other man, able to control. As one read the testimony, the one dominant impression it made on his mind was how small and weak and ineffectual even the strongest human life was, and how little was the effect that it could produce in what it was able to do in behalf of others.

How weak does even the strongest personality appear when contrasted with One Who can say such words as these I have just quoted! Suppose some great man now living were to say to us : "Come unto me, all ye that labour and are heavy laden, and I will give you rest. If any man thirst, let him come unto me, and drink. I am come that they may have life, and may have it abundantly," how startled we should be ! But

we have become familiar with the claim on the
lips of Christ and do not realize what we are
really confronted with in that single great Personality standing among men and offering to
meet the ultimate human need, to give us the
deepest, richest, most priceless thing in the
world, which no one of us can give another.
" I am come that ye may have life, and that ye
may have it abundantly."

And notice that here is not a claim only.
There is a strange and startling contrast. " The
thief cometh to steal, and to kill, and to destroy :
I am come that ye may have life." On the one
side is our Lord. Him we know. But who is
this thief on the other side who has come, not to
give life, but to reduce it, contract it, dilute it—
destroy it altogether? Well, we know well
enough that sin is such a thief, that wherever
sin is allowed to come into our lives it abridges
those lives, draws in the walls of their expansion,
cuts down and impoverishes their joys. And
there are many things short of sin, less coarse
and evil, which, nevertheless, draw in the boundaries of life, narrow and stifle it, and do the work
of the thief who came to kill, and to destroy, and
to steal. Over against all these He stands Who
said : " I came to give life, to give it abundantly."

Now we know very well what men and women
say when you bring them this offer of Christ's

about His life.   " Oh," they say, " it all depends
upon what you mean by life.   I have my own
idea of life.   The life I am living is rich and
satisfying to me, and I am not drawn to this life
that your tepid religion offers me in exchange."
But are those who answer so fully satisfied ?   Are
they really satisfied at all with any part of their
life except such of it as consists of the kind of
life that Jesus Christ our Lord Himself came to
bring, with which alone the hearts of men can be
content ?

What do we mean when we speak of life that
really satisfies us ?   I asked some boys a little
while ago what they meant when they spoke
about life, real life that would satisfy men.   Four
were boys at the Hill School, Pottstown, Pa.
They sat down and collaborated for a while as
to what real life meant to them, and when they
got through it came to this : Purity, integrity,
the principle of Christian service, unselfishness,
and the desire to be perfect.   I asked another
man at Princeton what life meant to him, real
life.   He was one of the best athletes in the college, and this was the answer he gave : Humility,
charitableness, bravery, strength of conviction,
honesty, sincerity, truthfulness and the power to
forgive.   I asked a man at Yale what he thought
life was.   He was the most popular man in the
senior class at that time.   This was what he
wrote down : " Service after the manner of Jesus,

honesty carried all the way through, sympathy, capacity for work, patience in holding to principle, as well as fidelity in actual duty."

Now if we were to define life better than these boys, and yet in the way they were feeling after, not in any concrete expressions, but in its central principle, we should borrow the words which Professor Drummond borrowed from Herbert Spencer. Spencer said that the perfect correspondence of any organism with its environment would be perfect life. Professor Drummond modified this by adding just one word : the perfect correspondence of any organism with a perfect environment would be perfect life. Or, to put it as it is stated in one of our best dictionaries : life is that state in any animal or plant in which its different functions are all occupied in active healthy expression. Now that is just what those boys were feeling after. Life is the free and fearless completion of ourselves. Life is our utter unfolding in the direction of that of which we are capable. Life is the pushing out of the rim of our world into the great and boundless riches of God. Life is the opening up of the gates of our prison house that we may go after Him Whose word to men was : "If ye abide in my word, then are ye truly my disciples ; and ye shall know the truth, and the truth shall make you free." Life is what Jesus Christ came to give, for His mission was this :

" The thief came to steal, and to kill, and to destroy. I am come that they may have life, and may have it abundantly."

One great purpose of the Incarnation was to show what we are in our deepest being in the purpose of God, and what we are capable of. Our Lord did not come to parade before men the exceptional life to which they could never attain. He came, as He Himself said, to show them what it had been His Father's will that they should all be. "As my Father hath sent me, even so send I you." "I go unto my Father. and your Father; and to my God, and your God." What Jesus Christ was in the fullness of His unlimited life was the revealing of what God has in His will for every one of us. The amplitudes that we see in Him, the subsidence of all the petty boundaries, the unhampered outgoing of His free spirit in the area of His Father, God, —all that is just a picture of what God meant the life of each one of us to be. That is why they called Him the Son of Man, because He was the picture of what God had meant that His son, man, might be.

And Christ came, not only to show the possibilities of such being, of what men could do and what they could be made, but to be Himself that expression of power in them competent to effect such a result, the tide of the boundless life flowing through all the channels that they could offer to Him. He came to be in mankind the deep, flowing stream of a new life. One regrets to find in some churches to-day in the repetition of the Apostles' Creed the omission of the sentence: " He descended into hell."   There is no word in the Creed which expresses more fully the uttermost reach of the purpose of our Lord and the scope and boundlessness of His love. Down even into hell He went in the utterance of His love for mankind. How much this means ! But to say no more, it means this, that deep into the dark of our human life He came, that there, below all sight, below all thought, He might release the vital streams that have been flowing from the fountain of Calvary ever since, and which have no other fountain.

We know what would happen in our bodies, to put it simply, if some great artery that fed our life were tied. Atrophy and palsy would creep at once over our unnourished frames. Precisely the same thing is true in the deeper life of our souls, if the arteries, those channels through which Christ would pour His energy and strength and power, are tied. To put the same thing still more simply : Suppose the Mississippi River instead of running into the Gulf ran out of the Gulf deep into the land. Suppose all of the rivers poured into the land instead of into the seas. As a matter of fact, that is in one sense what they do. We have got long past

looking at rivers as drains for the land. We
know that they are arteries through which the
life-blood of the seas flows upon the land by
way of the skies. And suppose there were no
Mississippi River. Suppose it were stopped at
the gate. What a chill and death would fall
upon the land! And how often that life of Christ
which comes up to the gates of men's lives is
stifled, the stream that would pour in kept out,
the power that would control and remake blocked
at the door through which it would enter. " The
thief is come," He says, "and you let him in, to
kill, and to steal, and to destroy ; I am come,
and you keep Me out. And I am come that
you may have life, and that you may have it in
all the abundance of God."

And we know that this life of Christ is real and
abundant life because it fulfills the tests of life.
It is a life of fullness in all its correspondences
and relationships. It completes life to the uttermost of its possibilities, setting it in all those ties
with that which is outside of it, which constitute
life. For, after all, there is no separable life.
All the life that we know is relationship. Our
Lord defined it in such terms in His great
prayer : "This is life eternal, that they might
know thee the only true God, and Jesus Christ,
whom thou hast sent." Life can only be construed in terms of correspondence.

We know that the life Christ came to give,

and does give, is the satisfying and real life, because it meets these testings. It gives us this wealth of correspondence of relationship.

> " Oh, the pure delight of a single hour,
>   That before Thy Cross I spend,
>   When I kneel in prayer, and with Thee, my God,
>   I commune as friend with friend."

We know that the life Christ brings is complete and full, because it reëstablishes the tie and union between ourselves and God, and He becomes to us again our Father and our Friend. We know it, because it is the root of all deep and true and satisfying human relationships. How can there be a real and full union of one man and one woman that is not a union in Christ? And for the highest friendship and its ideals we find sanction and nourishment best in Him and the groundwork of His life.

And Christ's is the real and satisfying life, because it is creative and energizing. It is not like the influence of that thief—selfishness, low desire, sin and small ambition—who kills and steals and destroys. But the life that Christ is teems with vitalizing power; it is strength and energy and new service in men. I have never seen it more beautifully put than in a letter of Stanley to David Livingstone. It was found by Lady Stanley in a little pocketbook which her husband had carried on the expedition for the relief of Livingstone. It was written in lead

pencil. It was a copy of the letter that Stanley
had written to the great explorer the very day
after he left him. It has sometimes been ques-
tioned whether Livingstone really made on Stanley the impression which Stanley describes in his
autobiography. There have been those who said
that that picture was but the reading back over
the intervening years of a growing hero worship.
But here is the letter which Stanley wrote as he
came fresh from the old missionary's companionship and the inspiration of his personality :

"My dear Doctor :

"I have parted from you all too soon ; I feel it
deeply ; I am entirely conscious of it from being so de-
pressed. . . .   In writing to you, I am not writing to
an idea now, but to an embodiment of warm, good fellowship, of everything that is noble and right, of sound common sense, of everything practical and right-minded.

"I have talked with you ; your presence is almost pal-
pable, though you are absent. . . .

"It seems as if I had left a community of friends and
relations. The utter loneliness of myself, the void that has
been created, the pang at parting, the bleak aspect of the
future, is the same as I have felt before, when parting from
dear friends.

"Why should people be subjected to these partings,
with the several sorrows and pangs that surely follow
them ?—It is a consolation, however, after tearing myself
away, that I am about to do you a service, for then I have
not quite parted from you ; you and I are not quite separate. Though I am not present to you bodily, you must

think of me daily until your caravan arrives. Though you are not before me visibly, I shall think of you constantly, until your least wish has been attended to. In this way the chain of remembrance will not be severed.

" 'Not yet,' I say to myself, ' are we apart,' and this to me, dear Doctor, is consoling, believe me. Had I a series of services to perform for you, why then ! we should never have to part.

" Do not fear then, I beg, to ask, nay, to command, whatever lies in my power. And do not, I beg of you, attribute these professions to interested motives, but accept them, or believe them, in the spirit in which they are made, in that true David Livingstone spirit I have happily become acquainted with."

And out from that lonely spot in eastern Africa, the younger man came to begin a new career; all the old aimlessness and shiftlessness and drifting gone forever from his life, to pass on now to lift up the mission which, beneath the dripping eaves of the hut in which he died, David Livingstone laid down. The tide of a new life and a new service was in him. " I came that ye may have life, and that ye may have it abundantly." He had seen Christ and felt the contagion of the life of Christ in Livingstone, and Christ's word, articulate or inarticulate, had come to live in him. And that life is life in the power and desire to serve.

This life that Christ came to give is the only real and satisfying life, because it alone endures. We gather at Northfield each summer and always go up to read afresh the brief inscription on Mr. Moody's grave on Round Top, " The world passeth away, and the lust thereof ; but he that doeth the will of God abideth forever."   We sing the same great truth constantly in George Matheson's hymn :

> " I lay in dust life's glory dead,
>   And from the ground there blossoms red
>   Life that shall endless be."

I wrote the other day to a friend about her sister-in-law's death, and this was the last sentence of the letter which she wrote in reply :

" I do not know if he "—that was her brother—" told you how beautiful it was at the last; how S——'s face lighted up with such an expression of surprise and adoration, with her eyes open to their fullest extent, and then it was all over.   Only a glimpse into the life that was not to end could have brought such a look to a human face."

" And that life," said He Who was the life, " I brought with Me and will give to you."

Let us lift our hearts to the life that shall endless be, to the liberty on which there never lay a chain, to the light of the land that hath no need of any sun, because the " Lamb is the light thereof," the land of the new morning and the tearless life. The thief cometh—let him not come in !—only to kill, and to steal, and to destroy. " I am come, and I stand at the door and ask you now to let Me in, that you may have life abundantly."

As these lectures close I would press all this in the most earnest and personal terms upon each one individually. The processes of social and moral progress in humanity are retarded or broken down because they are not carried on a volume of adequate spiritual life in men. There ought to be a Kingdom of Living Love and Brotherly Will on the earth. And some day there will be, but there is not now and there cannot be until the anemia of man is healed, and it can be healed in only one way—by more life in man, by life abounding in men. The commercial and materialistic solution of the world's problem has been fully tried. For a generation it has been preached and practiced as the one saving gospel and out of the depths to which it brought us we begin to turn heavenward again. The day for a new creed has dawned—the old creed of truth and hope and freedom and life, of the wealth and glory of a city unseen as yet, hid in the heavens and only possible on the earth as drawn down by men to whom the invisible things are the surest of all realities and who live and are strong in God.

Printed in the United States of America

ROBERT W. BOLWELL

After College—What?

12mo, cloth, net 75c.

A protest, in the form of autobiographical chapters, against dawdling through college. The author is sprightly and readable,—anything but preachy—but does put some very wholesome and helpful facts in such form as to grip the reader.

HALFORD E. LUCCOCK

Five-Minute Shop-Talks

12mo, cloth, net $1.00.

One of the best things of its kind yet issued. In each of these thirty or more brief addresses, Mr. Luccock employs terse, epigrammatic language and contrives to compress into a five-minute talk the wisdom and counsel of a fifty-minute sermon. Every word is made to tell—to tell something worth hearing and heeding.

CHARLES CARROLL ALBERTSON

Chapel Talks

A Collection of Sermons to College Students. 12mo, cloth, net $1.00.

Practical discourses on essential subjects delivered in various colleges and universities, including Columbia, Cornell, Dartmouth, Princeton, Yale, and Virginia. No one of these sermons required more than twenty-five minutes to deliver. They are characterized by earnest argument, familiar illustrations and forceful appeal.

CORTLANDT MYERS, D.D.   *Author of "Real Prayer," "The Real Holy Spirit," etc.*

The Man Inside

A Study of One's Self. By Minister at Tremont Temple, Boston. 12mo, cloth, net 50c.

A four-fold study of the inner life of a man, in which the popular pastor of Tremont Temple, discusses the forces that make him, lift him, save him, and move him. The book is prepared in bright, interesting fashion, and abundantly furnished with suitable and forceful illustration.

JOHN T. FARIS   *Popular-Price Editions*

The "Success Books"

Three Vols. each, formerly $1.25 net. Now each 60c. net (postage extra).

Seeking Success
Men Who Made Good
Making Good

Dr. J. R. Miller says: "Bright and short and full of illustrations from actual life, they are just the sort that will help young men in the home in school among associates and in business."

BIOGRAPHY

CHARLES G. TRUMBULL

Anthony Comstock, Fighter

Illustrated, 12mo, cloth, net $1.25.

An authorized biography of this great fighter for purity. The story is one of life-and-death adventure, moral and physical heroism, and incomparable achievement. During the thirty years in which Mr. Comstock has been working for the suppression of vice he has destroyed over 43 tons of vile books, 28,425 pounds of stereotype plates, two and a half million obscene pictures and 12,945 negatives. The detailed account of how all this was done is a most thrilling and remarkable story.

FRANK J. CANNON—DR. GEORGE L. KNAPP

Brigham Young and His Mormon Empire

Illustrated, 8vo, cloth, net $1.50.

Ex-Senator Cannon's personal acquaintance with this apostle of the Mormon Church and his knowledge of the religion and the people gained by having been born and brought up in the heart of Mormondom, give more than usual authority and interest to this biography. This life story of the man who founded a Mohammedan kingdom in a puritan republic sets forth in true perspective, in impartial and unbiased manner, the facts about one of the most romantic and interesting characters in American history.

FRANCES WILLARD

Frances Willard : Her Life and Her Work

By Ray Strachey. With an Introduction by Lady Henry Somerset. Illustrated, 8vo, cloth, net $1.50.

A notable new life of the great temperance advocate written by an English woman from an entirely new standpoint. Mrs. Strachey, the granddaughter of the author of "A Christian's Secret of a Happy Life," had immediate access to Miss Willard's letters, journals and papers, and the benefit of her grandmother's advice and knowledge.

Israel Zangwill says of the book, "A masterpiece of condensation, an adequate biography of perhaps the greatest woman America has produced. Nobody can read this book without becoming braver, better, wiser."

MRS. S. MOORE SITES

Nathan Sites :

Introduction by Bishop W. F. McDowell. Oriental Hand-Painted Illustrations, gilt top, net $1.50.

This is one of the notable books of the year. China looms large in current political and religious interest, so that this life story of one who for nearly half a century has been closely identified with social and religious reform in that country must have a large place in current literature.

JAMES H. SNOWDEN, D.D.

The Psychology of Religion

8vo, cloth, net $1.50.

Psychology is one of the most rapidly advancing of modern sciences, and Dr. Snowden's book will find a ready welcome. While especially adapted for the use of ministers and teachers, it is not in any sense an ultra-academic work. This is evidenced by the fact that the material forming it has been delivered not only as a successful Summer School course, but in the form of popular lectures, open to the general public.

WILLIAM HALLOCK JOHNSON, Ph.D., D.D.

Professor of Greek and New Testament Literature in Lincoln University, Pa.

The Christian Faith under Modern Searchlight

The L. P. Stone Lectures, Princeton. Introduction by Francis L. Patton, D.D. Cloth, net $1.25.

The faith which is to survive must not only be a traditional but an intelligent faith which has its roots in reason and experience and its blossom and fruit in character and good works. To this end, the author examines the fundamentals of the Christian belief in the light of to-day and reaches the conclusion that every advance in knowledge establishes its sovereign claim to be from heaven and not from men.

ANDREW W. ARCHIBALD, D.D.

Author of "The Bible Verified," "The Trend of the Centuries," etc.

The Modern Man Facing the Old Problems

12mo, cloth, net $1.00.

A thoughtful, ably-conducted study in which those problems of human life, experience and destiny, which, in one form or another, seem recurrent in every age, are examined from what may be called a Biblical viewpoint. That is to say, the author by its illuminating rays, endeavors to find elucidation and solution for the difficulties, which in more or less degree, perplex believer and unbeliever alike.

NOLAN RICE BEST   *Editor of "The Continent"*

Applied Religion for Everyman

12mo, cloth, net $1.00.

Nolan Rice Best has earned a well-deserved reputation in the religious press of America, as a writer of virile, trenchantly-phrased editorials. The selection here brought together represent his best efforts, and contains an experienced editor's suggestions for the ever-recurrent problems confronting Church members as a body, and as individual Christians. Mr. Best wields a facile pen, and a sudden gleam of beauty, a difficult thought set in a perfect phrase, or an old idea invested with new meaning and grace, meets one at every turn of the page."—*The Record Herald.*

JOHN W. LIGON   *Pastor Christian Church,*
Barboursville, Ky.

Paul the Apostle

12mo, cloth, net $1.15.

A life of the Apostle to the Gentiles, which, while fuller than the brief outlines usually followed in class instruction, is sufficiently condensed to admit of its being specially adapted to the use of busy men and women and the young people of the Church. The events and incidents of Paul's career are woven into a continuous narrative, furnishing a living picture of his wonderful life as far as that life can be known.

DWIGHT GODDARD

Jesus

And the Problems of Human Life. Cloth, net 50c.

These discourses show the value and usefulness of the Good News of a Spiritual Realm and the Way of Salvation to anyone who has felt a desire to make that supreme adventure in faith. They set the "Good News" into its right relation with present-day thought.

The Good News

Of a Spiritual Realm. Paraphrased by Dwight Goddard. *Second Edition.* 12mo, cloth, net $1.00.

An interweaving and paraphrasing of the Four Gospels, bringing out clearly the unity and reasonableness of Jesus' Life and Teachings. Appropriate for devotional reading, study classes, and as a gift book to those we would like to become interested in our Lord.

B. H. CARROLL, D.D.

An Interpretation of the English Bible

NEW VOLUMES ADDED TO THIS SERIES

The Pastoral Epistles of Paul and 1 and 2 Peter, Jude and 1, 2 and 3 John. 8vo, cloth, net $1.75.
The Book of Daniel and the Inter-Biblical Period. 8vo, cloth, net $1.75.
The Four Gospels. Vol. I. 8vo, cloth, net $2.50.
The Four Gospels. Vol. II. 8vo, cloth, net $2.50.
The Acts. 8vo, cloth, net $2.25.
James I-II, Thessalonians I and II Corinthians. Net $1.75.

"These works are designed especially for class use in the Seminary, Christian Colleges and Bible Schools, as well as the Sunday School. That they will make the greatest commentary on the English Bible ever published, is our sincere conviction."—*Baptist and Reflector.*

EDWARD AUGUSTUS GEORGE

The Twelve : Apostolic Types of Christian Men

12mo, cloth, net $1.15.
"Under his living touch the apostles seem very much like the men we know and their problems not dissimilar to our own."—*Congregationalist.*

PROF. W. G. MOOREHEAD

OUTLINE STUDIES in the NEW TESTAMENT SERIES

The Catholic Epistles and Revelation

In One Volume. *New Edition.* 12mo, net $1.20
Containing James, I and II Peter, I, II and III John, and Jude, and the Book of Revelation.

ALEXANDER CRUDEN

Complete Concordance

Large 8vo, cloth, net $1.25.
New Unabridged Edition, with the Table of Proper Names entirely revised and mistranslations in the meanings corrected, many suggestive notes.

WILLIAM SMITH, LL.D.

A Dictionary of the Bible

Its Antiquities, Biography, Geography and Natural History, with Numerous Illustrations and Maps. *A New Worker's Edition.* 776 pages. Net $1.25.

NEW THIN PAPER EDITION

The Boy Scouts' Twentieth Century New Testament

Officially authorized by the Boy Scouts' of America. New Thin Paper Edition.
181. 16mo, khaki cloth, net 85c.
182. 16mo, ooze leather, khaki color, net $1.50.
Contains an introduction by the Executive Board, the Scouts' Oath, and the Scouts' Law.

HENRY T. SELL, D.D. (Editor)
Author of
Sell's Bible Studies

XX Century Story of the Christ

12mo, cloth, net 60c.
From the text of The Twentieth Century New Testament, Dr. Sell has completed a Harmony of The Gospels which, while studiously avoiding repetition omits no important word in the fourfold record of the earthly life and teaching of our Lord. He has done his work well, and the result is a compilation specially designed and adapted for the use of the average reader.

ALBERT L. VAIL

Portraiture of Jesus in the Gospels

12mo, cloth, net 75c.

A fourfold portrait of Jesus as He stands out on the canvas of each of the Four Gospels. The varying and distinctive shadings of the four pictures, are not, Mr. Vail contends, a matter of accident but of Divine arrangement and design. Our Lord is thus presented in a fourfold aspect in order that His appeal to various classes of mankind might be the more manifold.

FRANK E. WILSON, B.D.

Contrasts in the Character of Christ

12mo, cloth, net $1.00.

Jesus Christ is still the key to the modern situation. No matter what "up-to-date" methods of reform and reclamation spring to life, the message of Christ is the one great solution of the problems confronting humanity. From this position Dr. Wilson leads his readers to a contemplation of an abiding Jesus, and to a consideration of many modern points of contact contained in His all-sufficient Gospel.

WILLIAM BRUCE DOYLE

The Holy Family

As Viewed and Viewing in His Unfolding Ministry. 12mo, cloth, net 75c.

This book covers new ground: for although separate sketches of individual members of Joseph's family abound, a study of the family group as a whole,—one marked with satisfactory detail remained to be furnished. This has been ably supplied. The author's work is everywhere suffused with reverence, as becometh one writing of some of the most endeared traditions cherished by the human race.

BOOKLETS

DAVID DE FOREST BURRELL   **Author of "The Gift"**

The Lost Star

An Idyll of the Desert. 16mo, net 35c.

An appealing story of a Shepherd's search for the Star. It is so tender, so sweet, so Christ-like, it is sure to captivate everyone.